An Important Message to Our Readers

This product provides information and general advice about the law. But laws and procedures change frequently, and they can be interpreted differently by different people. For specific advice geared to your specific situation, consult an expert. No book, software or other published material is a substitute for personalized advice from a knowledgeable lawyer licensed to practice law in your state.

3rd edition

Nolo's
Patents for
Beginners

by Attorneys David Pressman
and Richard Stim

NOLO

Keeping Up-to-Date

To keep its books up-to-date, Nolo issues new printings and new editions periodically. New printings reflect minor legal changes and technical corrections. New editions contain major legal changes, major text additions or major reorganizations. To find out if a later printing or edition of any Nolo book is available, call Nolo at 510-549-1976 or check our website at www.nolo.com.

To stay current, follow the "Update" service at our website at www.nolo.com/lawstore/update/list.cfm. In another effort to help you use Nolo's latest materials, we offer a 35% discount off the purchase of the new edition of your Nolo book when you turn in the cover of an earlier edition.

THIRD EDITION	JULY 2002
Editor	RICHARD STIM
Cover Design	SUSAN PUTNEY
Book Design	TERRI HEARSH
Proofreading	SHERYL ROSE
Index	JANET PERLMAN
Printing	BERTELSMANN SERVICES, INC.

Pressman, David, 1937–
   Nolo's patents for beginners/by David Pressman and Richard Stim.-- 3rd ed.
     p. cm.
   Includes index.
   ISBN 0-87337-850-4
    1. Patent laws and legislation--United States--Popular works. 2. Patent practice--United Staters--Popular works. I. Title: Patents for beginners. II. Stim, Richard. III. Title.

KF3114.6 .P737 2002
346.7304'86--dc21

                      20020741778

For information on bulk purchases or corporate premium sales, please contact the Special Sales Department. For academic sales or textbook adoptions, ask for Academic Sales. Call 800-955-4775 or write to Nolo, 950 Parker Street, Berkeley, CA 94710.

Acknowledgments

We would like to thank the knowledgeable and helpful staff at Nolo: Nolo production, sales and marketing, public relations and customer service departments.

Table of Contents

2 Qualifying for a Patent

3 Invention Documentation

4 Patent Searching

5 Reading and Writing Patents

10 Help Beyond This Book

Glossary

Index

Introduction

The principles of patent protection have changed little since 1790. If you devise a novel invention and qualify for a patent, you can, for a limited time, prevent anyone else from making, selling, or using it. For two centuries, businesses and inventors have used patent protection for products, processes, plants, and designs. However, the technological changes of the past 20 years have dramatically altered the patent landscape. The number of utility patent applications has nearly tripled since 1980. As of 2000, the United States Patent and Trademark Office (PTO) had issued over six million utility patents.

The explosive growth in biotechnology, information exchange, and the advent of business method and software patents has resulted in more patents being issued than ever before. Patents are now considered an integral part of a corporation's strategic business plan. And this strategy is not limited to corporate boardrooms. For example, the total revenue from patents for non-profit universities has gone from less than one million dollars in 1980 to over half a billion dollars today.

At the same time, the Internet is creating new avenues of public access to the patent application process. Anyone with an Internet connection can now search patent records at the PTO. Patent forms and rules can now be easily downloaded. Moreover, the first electronic filing of a utility patent occurred in 2000. Even more importantly, the dramatic advances in technology around the globe have been an incentive to getting new changes in U.S. patent law off the ground.

To stay current with the modern world of patents, we have a created a compact modern patent guide that explains patent law and provides clear instructions for deciphering and searching for patents. This book is intended for use by inventors, educators, entrepreneurs, students, and business people who must deal with and understand basic principles of patent law.

A. Organization of Text

Chapters are organized into four categories: basic patent principles, rules for documenting and acquiring patent rights, patent ownership and disputes, and international patent law. Chapter 10 provides helpful resources.

- **Principles of Patent Law.** The first two chapters explain basic patent principles, the types of patents, what can and cannot be protected, novelty, nonobviousness, and the statutory standards for patent protection.
- **Documenting, Searching, and Prosecuting Patents.** Chapters 3 through 6 deal with the invention process and the manner in which patents are granted by the PTO. Chapter 3 describes invention documentation. Chapter 4 describes patent searching, and Chapter 5 describes how to read and write a patent application. Chapter 6 describes patent prosecution—the

process of shepherding the patent application through the PTO.

- **Ownership and Patent Disputes.** Chapters 7 and 8 discuss the ownership and protection of patents. Chapter 7 provides information about ownership rights (for example, how inventors claim joint ownership and its implications). Chapter 8 focuses on the issues of litigating patent disputes and standards for patent infringement.
- **International Law.** Chapter 9 provides rules for international patent protection.
- **Resources.** We have provided a Glossary to assist in deciphering patent law. Additionally, Chapter 10: Help Beyond This Book, offers additional inventor and patent resources.

In order to function as an educational tool and desktop reference, this book filters complex material into readable segments. For instance, important rules regarding nonobviousness, novelty, and infringement are summarized and isolated throughout many chapters. In this manner, the reader is better able to easily find and digest rules and procedures.

An instructor using the book as a teaching tool can proceed systematically through the chapters beginning with principles of protection, followed by patent application principles and culminating with patent disputes and international patent law. For students, the material includes current case law, references, and examples.

Readers seeking a practical application of patent law will find detailed information on important patent procedures, including electronic patent searching, patent preparation, and international patent law. There are also extensive Internet references and resources.

B. Icons Used in This Book

To aid you in using this book, we use the following icons:

 The caution icon warns you of potential problems.

 This icon indicates that the information is a useful tip.

 This icon refers you to helpful books or other resources. ■

Chapter 1

Patents and Intellectual Property Law

The underlying principle of patents is that our nation rewards people who create useful things that are not obvious by giving inventors a monopoly over the sale and manufacture of their inventions. For example, in the 19th Century, one company controlled the manufacture and sale of all matches, while another company controlled the manufacture and sale of all safety pins. Matches and safety pins, just like paperclips and ballpoint pens, may seem obvious now, but a century ago they were novel discoveries and both of these items were protected by patent laws. Eventually all patents expire, and as a result, now any company can manufacture and sell matches and safety pins without seeking permission.

This chapter will introduce you to some patent basics and summarize patent standards. Since patents are a member of the intellectual property family, we will also introduce principles of copyrights, trademarks, and trade secrets.

Definitions, Caselaw and Statutes

We define many terms throughout this book and these definitions are collected in the Glossary at the end of this book. We also provide references to lawsuits and statutes. You can recognize the reference to lawsuits because the names are in italic usually separated by a "v," for example, *Diamond v. Chakrabarty*, 447 U.S. 303 (1980). The information following the names refers to volume, book and page number where the case is located. The citation system is beyond the scope of this book, but if you are interested in doing further legal research, read *Legal Research: How to Find & Understand the Law*, by Stephen Elias and Susan Levinkind (Nolo). A statute is another form of legal citation and is recognizable by the use of a section mark ("§"), for example, 35 U.S.C. § 161. The patent statutes passed by Congress can be found in Title 35 of the United States Code (U.S.C.). The U.S.C. can be found in most law libraries and the entire patent code is available at the U.S. Patent and Trademark Office website, www.uspto.gov.

A. What Is a Patent?

A patent is a grant from the federal government that gives an inventor the right to exclude others from making, using, selling, importing, or offering an invention for sale for a fixed period of time. For example, Whitcomb Judson received a patent in 1893 for the zipper, and for 17 years, Judson alone was entitled to manufacture and sell this invention.

"Invention" has a broad meaning. It is any new article, machine, composition, process, or new use developed by a human. For example, in 1988 Drs. Leder and Stewart (on behalf of Harvard University) were issued the first patent for a new animal life form embodied in a genetically altered mouse. This new life form is an invention.

The patent right lasts for approximately 17 to 18 years, provided certain fees are paid. After the patent right ends, anyone can freely copy the invention.

A patent is a form of personal property and can be sold outright for a lump sum, or its owner can give anyone permission to use the invention ("license it") in return for royalty payments. A patent can also be transferred by gift, will, or descent under a state's intestate succession (no-will) laws.

B. The Three Types of Patents

There are three types of patents—utility patents, design patents, and plant patents.

Utility Patents: A utility patent, the most common type of patent, covers inventions that function in a unique manner to produce a utilitarian result. Examples of utility inventions are Velcro fasteners, new drugs, electronic circuits, software, semiconductor manufacturing processes, new bacteria, new animals, plants, automatic transmissions, and virtually anything else under the sun that can be made by humans. This book is devoted primarily to utility patents.

Design Patents: A design patent covers the unique, ornamental, or visible shape or design of a non-natural object. Thus if a lamp, a building, a computer case, or a desk has a truly unique shape, its design can be patented. Even computer screen icons can be patented. However, the uniqueness of the shape must be purely ornamental or aesthetic; if the shape is *functional* and aesthetic, then only a utility patent is proper. A useful way to distinguish between a design and a utility invention is to ask, "Will removing the novel features substantially affect the function of the device?" For example, removing the carved wood design in the headboard of a bed. The headboard design would not affect how the bed functioned and could be protected as a design patent. On the other hand, a baseball bat and fishing rod may have pleasing designs but unless they have non-functional aesthetic features, their shape is purely functional and suitable only for a utility patent. (For more information on design patents, see Chapter 2, Section F.)

Plant Patents: A plant patent covers plants that can be reproduced through the use of grafts and cuttings such as flowers. These are referred to as asexually reproducible plants. (35 U.S.C. § 161) The Plant Variety Protection Act covers those plants that use pollination (sexually reproducible plants). (7 U.S.C. § 2321.) Under some circumstances, utility patents can cover sexually and asexually reproducible plants. (For more information on plant patents, see Chapter 2.)

Patent rights extend throughout the entire U.S., its territories, and possessions. Under international treaties, the owner of a U.S. patent can acquire patent rights in other countries by filing corresponding patent applications abroad as outlined in Chapter 9. Congress derives its power to make the patent statutes from the U.S. Constitution (Art. 1, Sec. 8). The statutes, in turn, authorize the PTO to issue its Rules of Practice and its *Manual of Patent Examining Procedure* (MPEP).

C. Patent Rights

A patent gives its owner the right to sue infringers, that is, anyone who imports, makes, uses, sells or offers the invention for sale (or an essential part of it) without authorization. If the patent owner wins the lawsuit, the judge will issue a signed order (an "injunction") against the infringer, ordering the infringer not to make, use, or sell the invention any more. The judge will also award the patent owner damages—money to compensate the patent owner for loss due to the infringement. The amount of the damages is often equivalent to a reasonable royalty (say 5%), based on the infringer's sales. However, if the patent owner can convince the judge that the infringer acted in bad faith—for example, infringed intentionally with no reasonable excuse—the judge can triple the damages and make the infringer pay the patent owner's attorney fees. (For more information on patent infringement, see Chapter 8.)

Offensive Rights—Not Protection

Many people refer to patents as a form of "protection." However, patents don't provide any defensive "protection" in their own right. A patent is an offensive weapon. For example, patent ownership, by itself, will not necessarily keep anyone from copying your invention and violating your patent rights. However, as a patent owner, you can successfully sue or threaten to sue anyone who wrongfully trespasses on those rights. The distinction between defensive and offensive rights is as important in intellectual property law as it is in football or basketball: while a good defense may be valuable, the patent owner will need to use the patent's powerful offense to win the game or stop the infringer.

D. The Requirements for Obtaining a Patent

An inventor applies for the patent by filing a patent application, a set of papers that describes an invention. The Patent and Trademark Office (PTO) is a division of the Department of Commerce. A patent examiner at the PTO must be convinced that the invention claimed in the application satisfies the "novelty" and "nonobviousness" requirements of the patent laws.

The novelty requirement is easy to satisfy: the invention must be different from what is already known to the public. Any difference, however slight, will suffice. In addition to being novel, the examiner must also be convinced that the invention is nonobvious (or unobvious). This means that at the time the inventor came up with the invention, it would not have been considered obvious to a person skilled in the technology (called "art"). Unobviousness is best shown by new and unexpected, surprising, or far superior results, when compared to previous inventions and knowledge ("prior art") in the particular area of the invention. In addition to being novel and unobvious, utility inventions must also meet other legal requirements. More on this in Chapter 2.

We discuss the patent application process and the PTO in more detail in Chapters 5 and 6, and information about the PTO can accessed online at www.uspto.gov or by writing to the Commissioner for Patents, Washington, DC 20231.

E. How Long Do Patent Rights Last?

Until recently, utility patents were granted for a period of 17 years, assuming required maintenance fees were paid. However, as a result of a change in patent laws, utility, and plant patents issuing from applications filed after June 7, 1995, will expire 20 years from the date of filing. However, certain utility patents will be extended to compensate for the following:

- delays resulting from the failure of the PTO to examine a new application within 14 months of filing
- delays caused by the PTO's failure to issue a patent within three years from filing, unless the delay was caused or instigated by the inventor, and
- delays caused by the PTO's failure to take certain office actions for more than four months.

In addition, patent rights may be extended for certain products whose commercial marketing has been delayed due to regulatory review, such as for drugs or food additives. (35 U.S.C. §§ 155-156.)

The term for design patents is 14 years from the date the patent is issued (the "date of issue").

From the date of filing to the date of issuance (the "pendency period") the inventor has no patent rights. However, when and if the patent later issues, the inventor will obtain the right to prevent the continuation of any infringing activity that started during the pendency period. In some cases, if the application has been published, the applicant may later seek royalties for infringements during the pendency period. Patents aren't renewable, and once patented, an invention may not be repatented.

F. How Patent Rights Can Be Lost

Patent rights can be lost if:

- fees required to keep the patent in force (known as "maintenance fees") aren't paid (see Chapter 6)
- it can be proved that the patent doesn't (a) adequately explain how to make and use the invention, (b) improperly describes the invention, or (c) contains claims that are inadequate (see Chapter 5)
- one or more earlier patents or other publications (prior-art references) are uncovered which show that the invention wasn't new or wasn't different enough to qualify for patent rights (see Chapter 4)
- the patent owner engages in certain defined types of illegal conduct, that is, commits antitrust or other violations connected with the patent (see Chapter 8), or
- the patent applicant committed "fraud on the Patent and Trademark Office (PTO)" by failing to disclose material information, such as relevant prior-art references, to the PTO during the period when the patent application was pending (see Chapter 8).

In short, the patent monopoly, while powerful, may be defeated and is limited in scope and time.

G. Intellectual Property— The Big Picture

Intellectual property refers to any product of the human mind or intellect, such as an idea, invention, artistic expression, unique name, business method, industrial process, or chemical formula. Intellectual property (IP) law determines when and how a person can capitalize on a creation. Over the years, intellectual property law has fallen into several distinct subcategories, according to the type of "property" involved:

- **Patent Law** deals with the protection of the mental concepts or creations known as inventions.
- **Trademark Law** deals with the protection of a brand name, design, slogan, sound, smell, or any other symbol used to identify and market goods or services. Examples of trademarks are the words Ivory, Coke, and Nolo, as well as the Mercedes-Benz star, and the NBC chimes.
- **Copyright Law** grants to authors, composers, programmers, artists, and the like the right to prevent others from copying or using their works without permission and to recover damages from those who do so. For example, copyright law gives an author offensive rights against anyone who copies her book without permission.

- **Trade Secret Law** protects confidential business information that gives a business a competitive business advantage over its competitors—for example, manufacturing processes, magic techniques, and formulae.
- **Unfair Competition Law** permits a business to sue over certain types of unethical behavior by competitors. For example, if a company claims to be an authorized "Maytag" dealer but is not; or if car company imitates a singer's unique vocal style in a car commercial to imply the singer endorses the car.

H. Trademarks

Trademarks are the most familiar branch of intellectual property law. On a daily basis, everyone sees, uses, and makes many decisions on the basis of trademarks. For instance, the purchase of a car, an appliance, packaged food, a magazine, computer, or a watch, is based, at least to some extent, on the trademark.

1. What Is a Trademark?

In its most literal meaning, a trademark is any word or other symbol that is consistently associated with a product or service and identifies and distinguishes that product or service from others in the marketplace. A trademark can be a word (Kodak), a design

or logo (the AT&T bell), a sound (the NBC chimes), shapes (the truncated, contrasting, conical top of Cross pens), colors (and color combinations), and even smells. The term "trademark" is also commonly used to mean "service marks." These are marks (words or other symbols) that are associated with services offered in the marketplace. The letters CBS in connection with the broadcast network are one example of a service mark. Another is the emblem used by Blue Cross–Blue Shield for its medical insurance services.

2. Trademark Rights and Registration

The trademark owner can prevent another business from using the same or a confusingly similar mark for the same or similar goods. Owners of famous marks can prevent the use of similar marks that dilute or tarnish the trademark's image, even if these uses are not on similar goods or services.

Contrary to popular belief, trademarks do not have to be registered for offensive rights to be acquired (although registration can substantially add to the trademark owner's rights). Trademark rights are acquired by the first person to actually use the trademark in commerce or file an intent-to-use (ITU) application to register the trademark and subsequently use the mark in commerce. Actual use in commerce means shipping goods or advertising services in interstate or foreign commerce that bear the trademark.

3. Relationship of Trademark Law to Patent Law

Trademarks are useful in conjunction with inventions, whether patentable or not. For example, consider the Crock Pot and the Hula Hoop. Both of these products were unpatentable, but the names of the products were protected under trademark laws. As a result of advertising consumers sought out the trademarked products and not those from competitors. In short, a trademark provides brand-name recognition to the product and a patent provides a tool to enforce a monopoly based on functional features. Since trademark rights can be kept forever (as long as the trademark continues to be used), a trademark can be a powerful means of effectively extending a monopoly on the market for the invention long after the patent has expired. For example, the Scotchguard process for protecting carpets was invented by Patsy Sherman & Samuel Smith and patented in 1973. Even though other companies may now copy the process, the Scotchguard trademark is still synonymous with quality carpet protection and gives the company an edge among consumers who want products to protect carpet and fabrics.

For more information on federal trademarks, access the U.S. Trademark Office at www.uspto.gov, write to Commissioner of Trademarks, Washington, DC 20231, or review *Trademark: Legal Care for Your Business & Product Name*, by Stephen Elias (Nolo).

Trademarks and Trade Names

A trade name is a word or words under which a company does business, while a trademark is the word or other symbol under which a company sells its products or services. For example, the words Procter & Gamble are a trade name, while Ivory is a trademark, that is, a brand name for Procter & Gamble's white soap. Many companies such as Ford, use the same words as a trade name and a trademark, so sometimes the difference becomes academic.

I. Copyright

In this section copyright law is explained and distinguished from patents. Information is provided about acquiring and maintaining copyright. Some specific types of works that are covered by copyright are books, poetry, plays, songs, catalogs, photographs, computer programs, advertisements, labels, movies, maps, drawings, sculpture, prints and art reproductions, board games and rules, and recordings.

1. What Is a Copyright?

Copyright is a legal right given to an author, artist, composer, or programmer, to exclude others from publishing or copying literary, dramatic, musical, artistic, or software works. A copyright covers only the author's or artist's particular way of expressing an idea. While a copyright can provide offensive rights on the particular arrangement of words that constitute a book or play, it can't cover the book's subject matter, message, or teachings. For example, you are free to publish any of the ideas, concepts, and information in this (or any) book, provided that you use your own words. But if you copy the specific wording, then you have infringed the copyright on this book.

To obtain a copyright, a work must be "original," not merely the result of extended effort. For example, a telephone company that compiled, through much work, an alphabetical directory of names and addresses could not prevent another publisher from copying the directory, since it had no originality. Certain items, such as a title, short phrase, lettering, an idea, a plan, a form, a system, a method, a process, a concept, a principle, and a device can't be covered through copyright. U.S. government publications, by law, aren't covered by copyright and may almost always be freely copied and sold by anyone, if desired. Copyright can't be used for a utilitarian article, unless it has an aesthetic feature that can be separated from and can exist independently of the article (known as the "separability requirement"). For example, copyright cannot protect a belt buckle but can protect a design that is affixed to the buckle.

2. Rights and Registration

The copyright springs into existence the instant the work of expression first assumes some tangible form, for example, once a song is recorded or a book is written. Copyright lasts for the life of the author plus 70 years, or for works made for hire, 95 years from publication or 120 years from creation, whichever is shorter. A work made for hire is one made by an employee in the course of the employment or by an independent contractor under a written work-made-for-hire contract. The copyright owner in a work made for hire is the hiring party or employer.

Registration is not necessary to acquire copyright protection but if it is accomplished within three months of the time the item is distributed or published, or before the infringement occurs, it may entitle the copyright owner to attorney fees, costs, and damages that don't have to be proved (called "statutory damages").

 Copyright Notice. While no longer necessary for works published after March 1, 1989, it's still advisable to place the familiar copyright notice (for example, Copyright © 2001 David Pressman) on each published copy of the work. This tells anyone who sees the work that the copyright is being claimed, who is claiming it, and when the work was first published. This notice prevents an infringer from later claiming that the infringement was accidental.

3. Copyright Compared With Utility Patent

Things that are entitled to a patent are generally not entitled to a copyright, and vice versa. Assuming they don't have any aesthetic components, patents are exclusive for machines, compositions, articles of manufacture, processes, and new uses. On the other hand, copyrights are exclusive for works of expression, such as writings, movies, plays, recordings, and artwork, assuming they don't have any functional aspects. However, a few creations may be eligible for both types of coverage (see Computer Software sidebar, below).

In many areas, both forms of coverage can be used together for different aspects of the creation. For instance, in a parlor game, the game apparatus, if sufficiently unique, can be patented, while the gameboard, rules, box, and design of the game pieces can be covered by copyright. The artwork on the box or package for almost any invention can be covered by copyright, as can the instructions accompanying the product. Also the name of the game (for example, Dungeons and Dragons) is a trademark and can be covered as such.

Computer Software

Viewed one way, computer programs are nothing more than a series of numerical relationships (termed "routines") and as such cannot qualify for a patent, although they can be covered under the copyright laws because they constitute a creative work of expression. However, viewed from another perspective, computer programs are a set of instructions that make a machine (the computer) operate in a certain way. In recent years, many patents have been issued on computer programs where the program affected some hardware or process or performed some commercially useful function. When choosing whether to rely on copyright or a patent for software, the software author must weigh the broader offensive rights that a patent brings against the expense and time in obtaining one. Likewise, the ease with which copyright is obtained must be counterbalanced by the narrow nature of its coverage.

4. Copyright Compared With Design Patents

There's considerable overlap here, since aesthetics are the basis of both forms of coverage. Design patents are used mainly to cover industrial designs where the shape of the object has ornamental features and the shape is inseparable from, or meaningless if separated from, the object. For example, a tire tread design and a computer case are perfect for design patents. However, a surface decal, which could be used elsewhere, is not.

Copyright, on the other hand, can be used for almost any artistic or written creation, whether or not it's inseparable from an underlying object, so long as the aspect of the work for which copyright is being sought is ornamental and not functional. This means copyright can be used for pure surface ornamentation, such as the artwork on a can of beans, as well as sculptural works where the "art" and the object are integrated, such as a statue. For instance, the shape of a toy was held to be properly covered by copyright since the shape played no role in how the toy functioned and since a toy wasn't considered to perform a useful function (although many parents who use toys to divert their children would disagree).

Compared to copyright, design patents are relatively expensive and time-consuming to obtain and the rights last only 14 years. However, a design patent offers broader rights than a copyright in that it covers the aesthetic principles underlying the design. This means that someone else coming up with a similar, but somewhat changed design would probably be liable for design patent infringement.

For more information on copyright, read *The Copyright Handbook*, by Stephen Fishman (for written works), *Copyright Your Software*, by Stephen Fishman (for software and computer-related expressions), and *Web and Software Development: A Legal Guide*, also by Stephen Fishman. Nolo publishes all three books. Also, the Copyright Office, Washington, DC 20559, provides free information and copyright forms at www.loc.gov, or call 202-707-9100.

J. Trade Secrets

Here we provide a basic definition of trade secrets, distinguish trade secret protection from patents, list the advantages and disadvantages of trade secret versus patenting, and explain how to acquire and maintain trade secret rights.

1. What Is a Trade Secret?

A trade secret is any information, design, device, process, composition, technique, or formula that is not known generally and that affords its owner a competitive business advantage. Examples of trade secrets are a chemical formula, a manufacturing process, a "magic-type" secret (such as techniques used to produce laser light shows and fireworks), and a recipe. Since these types of information and know-how go to the very heart of a business's competitive position, businesses expend a great deal of time, energy, and money to guard their trade secrets.

2. Acquiring and Maintaining Trade Secret Rights

The trade secret owner need only take reasonable precautions to keep the information confidential in order to acquire and maintain trade secret rights. Also, an employer should have all employees who have access to company trade secrets sign an agreement to keep the information confidential. Over the years the courts have devised a number of tests for determining what these reasonable precautions should be and whether a trade secret owner has taken them. Most states now have a statute that makes the theft of a trade secret a criminal offense as well as the basis for civil lawsuit (for instance, the Uniform Trade Secrets Act, California Civil Code § 3246 et seq.). Moreover, there is now a federal statute for the same purpose (Economic Espionage Act, 18 U.S.C. §1831 et seq.).

3. Trade Secrets Compared With Patents

Assuming that an invention has been kept secret, an inventor can rely on trade secret principles to enforce rights on the invention. If an invention is maintained as a trade secret and put into commercial use, the in-

ventor must file a patent application within one year of the date the invention was used commercially. If the inventor waits over a year, any patent that the inventor does ultimately obtain will be held invalid if this fact is discovered. More on this "one-year rule" in Chapter 2, Section D.

When a patent issues, the public has complete access to the ideas, techniques, approaches, and methods underlying the invention. This is because a patent application must clearly explain how to make and use the invention. Since the application is printed verbatim when the patent issues, all of this "know-how" becomes public. This public disclosure doesn't usually hurt the inventor, however, since the patent can be used to prevent anyone else from commercially exploiting the underlying information.

The PTO treats patent applications as confidential so it is possible to apply for a patent and still maintain the underlying information as a trade secret during the patent application process, at least for the first 18 months. (See Section 4.)

4. Loss of Trade Secret Rights As a Result of 18-Month Publication Rule

As a result of recent legislation, starting with applications filed November 29, 2000, every pending patent application will be published for the public to view 18 months after its filing date (or earlier if requested by the applicant). The only exception is if the applicant, at the time of filing, informs the PTO that the application will not be filed abroad. If the patent application is published but is later rejected then the inventor is in the unfortunate position of having lost both trade secret and patent rights.

If an inventor files a patent application on an invention and the inventor wants to keep it as a trade secret if the patent isn't granted, the inventor will have to take affirmative steps to withdraw the application before publication to prevent loss of the trade secret rights. (See Chapter 6.) There is one advantage to publication in that an applicant whose application is published may obtain royalties from an infringer from the date of the publication if the application later issues as a patent. The infringer must have had actual notice of the publication. This can be accomplished by sending a copy of the publication to an infringer.

5. Advantages of Trade Secret Protection

Some people choose trade secret rights over a patent, assuming it's possible to protect the creation by either. Let's look at some of the reasons why:

- The main advantage of a trade secret is the possibility of perpetual protection. While a patent is limited by statute to 20 years from filing and isn't renewable, a trade secret will last indefinitely if not discovered. For example, some fireworks and sewing needle trade secrets have been maintained for decades.

- A trade secret can be maintained without the cost or effort involved in patenting.

- There is no need to disclose details of the invention to the public for trade secret rights (as the inventor has to do with a patented invention).

- With a trade secret, the inventor has definite, already existing rights and doesn't have to worry about whether the patent application will be allowed.

- Since a trade secret isn't distributed to the public as a patent is, no one can look at the trade secret and try to design around it, as they can with the claims of a patent.

- A trade secret can be established without naming any inventors, as must be done with a patent application. Thus no effort need be made to determine the proper inventor and, provided it has its employees sign the usual employment agreement, a company needn't request its inventor-employee to assign (legally transfer) ownership of the trade secret to it, as is required with a patent application.

- A trade secret does not have to meet the novelty and nonobviousness requirements of a patent. In other words, it does not have to be as significant or important an advance as does a patented invention.

- A trade secret can cover more information, including many relatively minor details, whereas a patent generally covers but one broad principle and its ramifications. For example, a complicated manufacturing machine with many new designs and that incorporates several new techniques can be covered as a trade secret merely by keeping the whole machine secret. To cover it by patent, on the other hand, many expensive and time-consuming patent applications would be required, and even then the patent wouldn't cover many minor ideas in the machine.
- Trade secret rights are obtained immediately, whereas a patent takes a couple of years, in which time rapidly evolving technology can bypass the patented invention.

6. Disadvantages of Trade Secret

There are many circumstances in which the trade secret rights have important disadvantages. In these contexts, using patent rights is essential.

The main reason that trade secrets are often a poor way to cover the work is that they can't be maintained when the public is able to discover the information by inspecting, dissecting, or analyzing the product (called "reverse engineering"). Because very sophisticated analytic tools are now avail-able, most things can be analyzed and copied, no matter how sophisticated or small they are. And remember, the law generally allows anyone to copy and make anything freely, unless it is patented or subject to copyright coverage, or unless its shape is its trademark, such as the shape of the Fotomat huts.

Strict precautions must always be taken and continually enforced to maintain the confidentiality of a trade secret. If the trade secret is discovered legitimately, or by any other method, it's generally lost forever, although the trade secret owner does have rights against anyone who purloins the trade secret by illegal means.

A trade secret can be patented by someone else who discovers it by legitimate means. For instance, suppose an inventor creates a new formula for a hair treatment lotion, and someone who has never even heard of the lotion comes up with the same formula and patents it successfully. She can legitimately sue and hold the inventor liable for infringing her patent! Under new legislation, an inventor who has used a process has a defense to a claim of infringement by a second inventor who obtains a patent on the process, provided that the first inventor's use was over a year before the patent's filing date. (See Chapter 8, Section D.)

 For more information on trade secrets, consult *Nondisclosure Agreements: Protecting Your Trade Secrets and More*, by Richard Stim and Stephen Fishman (Nolo).

K. Unfair Competition

Unfair competition includes any number of devious methods by which businesses act unfairly, including false advertising claims, false endorsement of products, deceptive packaging, or dishonest promotions or marketing. The scope of unfair competition law is nebulous in the first place and is regularly being changed by judges who make new and often contradictory rulings.

The primary federal law used to enforce unfair competition law is the federal "false designation of origin" statute (15 U.S.C. §1125(a)). If an injured party can prove that a business has engaged in unfair competition, a judge will issue an injunction (legal order) prohibiting the business from any further such activity or defining what the business can and can't do. Further, the court may award compensation (monetary damages) to the injured business (that is, the business that lost profits because of the public's confusion). Unfair competition occasionally intersects with patents. For example, a company may advertise it has a superior patented process for roach killing when it does not have a patent. A competitor can sue to stop the false advertising. ■

Chapter 2

Qualifying for a Patent

Regardless of whether a new invention is a drug, a computer program or a golf club, the PTO requires that it meet four patent requirements. The invention must fit into one of the statutory classifications and it must be useful, novel, and nonobvious. In this chapter, we discuss these legal requirements and an important concept known as "prior art." This chapter primarily deals with the standards and requirements for utility patents. The legal requirements for design patents are discussed briefly in Section F and plant patents are discussed in Section G.

A. Legal Requirements for a Utility Patent

More than half of all inventions submitted to the PTO don't receive a patent. These inventions fail to meet one of the four patent requirements:

1. **Statutory Class.** The invention must fit into one of five classes established by Congress. (35 U.S.C. §101.) These classes are:
   - processes (method)
   - machines
   - articles of manufacture
   - compositions, or
   - "new uses" of one of the first four.
2. **Useful.** The invention must be useful. (35 U.S.C. §101.)
3. **Novelty.** The invention must be novel. That is, the invention must have an aspect that is different in some way

from all previous knowledge and inventions. (35 U.S.C. §102.)
4. **Nonobvious.** The invention must not be obvious from the standpoint of someone who has ordinary skill in the specific technology involved in the invention. (35 U.S.C. §103.)

Most inventions meet three of these standards; that is, they fit within at least one statutory class, have utility, and possess novelty. As a reflection of this, we have presented the four requirements in Fig. 2A, as three upward steps. The last requirement, nonobviousness, is represented by a relatively high step. That's because most of the inventions that fail to receive a patent are rejected because the PTO believes the invention is obvious.

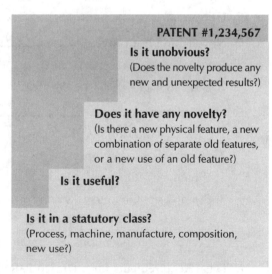

PATENT #1,234,567

Is it unobvious?
(Does the novelty produce any new and unexpected results?)

Does it have any novelty?
(Is there a new physical feature, a new combination of separate old features, or a new use of an old feature?)

Is it useful?

Is it in a statutory class?
(Process, machine, manufacture, composition, new use?)

**Fig. 2A—Patentability Mountain
The Four Legal Requirements for Getting a
Utility Patent**

The Inventor's Status Is Irrelevant

In discussing the requirements for obtaining a patent, we do not mention the inventor's status or personal qualifications because these are irrelevant. The applicant must qualify as a true inventor of the invention (discussed in Chapter 7) and personal qualities such as age, sex, citizenship, country of residence, mental competence, health, physical disabilities, incarceration, nationality, race, creed, and religion are irrelevant. Even dead or insane persons may apply through their personal representative. Similarly, the manner of making an invention is totally irrelevant to patentability. A child who discovers something by accident is treated the same as a genius who comes up with the idea through years of hard work.

B. Statutory Classes

To be patentable, an invention must be "statutory subject matter." This means that the invention must fall into one of the statutory classes. These statutory classes, although only five, are very comprehensive. The Supreme Court has stated that anything that is made by humans falls within these classes. Laws of nature, natural phenomena, and abstract ideas do not fall within these classes. (*Diamond v. Chakrabarty*, 447 U.S. 303 (1980).)

With a few exceptions that we'll discuss below, most inventions can be squeezed into at least one of the statutory classes, and in many instances an invention will fit into more than one. This overlap is not a problem, since an applicant for a patent is not required to specify the class in which an invention belongs. Below, we discuss the five statutory classes in more detail.

1. Statutory Classes: Processes, Including Software

Processes (sometimes referred to as "methods") are ways of doing or making things that involve more than purely mental manipulations. Processes always have one or more steps, each of which expresses some activity and manipulates or treats some physical thing. Purely manual processes, such as a method of gripping a golf club or a method of using a keyboard, were once regarded as unprotectible, but now these are being patented, provided they attain a useful result and are novel and unobvious.

a. Conventional Processes

Examples of conventional processes are heat treatments, chemical reactions for making or changing something, and ways of making products or chemicals. To give an example of an extreme process patent, consider a process of attaching a hairpiece to a bald person's scalp by putting suture anchors in the scalp and sewing the piece to the suture anchors.

b. Software Processes

A software program, if it is patentable, may fall in either the process class or machine class. Since most software-related inventions are claimed as processes, we'll discuss them first and discuss machine software patents in Section B2. To be classified as a process, a software program must affect some hardware or process, or must produce a useful, concrete, and tangible result. Examples include a program that analyzes EKG, spectrographic, seismic, or data bit signals; controls a milling machine; creates images on a computer screen; formats the printing of mathematical formulae; submits bids for a service online; calculates mutual fund values; or recognizes patterns or voices. However, if the software process merely crunches numbers, generates a curve, or calculates distances without any practical purpose, then it is not patentable.

Note that these rules are still evolving and the main patent court—the Court of Appeals for the Federal Circuit (CAFC)—determined that an algorithm for making a diagonal line on a monitor smoother is a patentable software process, probably because smoother diagonal lines look better and are easier to see. (*In re Alappat*, 33 F.3d 1526 (Fed. Cir. 1994).) The CAFC also held another patent valid—a general-purpose computer data structure that organizes information into different categories selected from an infinite number of categories. (*In re Lowry*, 32 F.3d 1579 (Fed. Cir. 1994).)

c. Business Methods and Processes

In 1998, the CAFC ruled that a software process that calculated mutual fund investments was valid. The ruling was groundbreaking because it established patent protection for a method of doing business and it legitimized software patents. Previously software could only be patented if the software resulted in some physical activity, for example a change of physical matter from one state to another. Now, a business software process or method is patentable if it is directed toward a "useful, concrete and tangible result." (*State Street Bank & Trust Co. v. Signature Financial Group, Inc.*, 149 F.3d 1368 (Fed. Cir. 1998).) The *State Street* ruling has prompted a large number of Internet-related patent filings, some of which have provoked controversy, for example Amazon.com's "one-click" patent for an express method of ordering merchandise online. Critics of business method patents argue that the PTO lacks the resources to properly evaluate relevant prior art. For more information on this debate, see www.bustpatents.com.

2. Statutory Classes: Machines

Machines are devices or things used for accomplishing a task. Like processes, they usually involve some activity or motion that's performed by working parts, but in machines, the emphasis is on the parts or hardware, rather than the activity. Another way of saying this is that a process involves the actual steps of manipulation while a machine is the thing that does the manipulating.

a. Conventional Machines

Examples of machines are cigarette lighters, robots, sewage treatment plants, clocks, all electronic circuits, automobiles, boats, rockets, telephones, TVs, computers, VCRs, disk drives, printers, lasers, and photocopiers. Many inventions can be claimed as a process or as a machine. For instance, a novel weaving machine can be claimed in terms of its actual hardware or as a process for weaving fabrics, provided the weaving process is novel.

b. Software Machines

Although most software inventions are claimed as processes, they can usually also be claimed as machines. Whether the software invention is categorized as a process or machine depends upon the way in which the invention is described in the claims section of the patent application. (The drafting of patent claims is discussed in Chapter 5.) If possible, both types of claims should usually be provided in a single patent application. This difference in the claims is really a simple change of language. The example below involves a software invention that controls a milling machine.

EXAMPLE: A system for controlling a milling machine can be claimed either as a process or a machine. As a process the system would be claimed as follows:

    a. measuring an object to obtain a set of measurements, and

    b. controlling a milling machine according to the set of measurements.

As a machine the system would be claimed as follows:

    a. means [or an apparatus] for measuring an object to obtain a set of measurements, and

    b. means [or an apparatus] for adjusting a milling machine according to the set of measurements.

Note that the first step or means for measuring can be regarded as either an action or as the hardware for performing the action. This applies equally to the second step.

3. Statutory Classes: Manufactures

Manufactures, sometimes termed "articles of manufacture," are simple items that have been made by human hands or by machines. Most manufactures have few or no working or moving parts as prime features. Examples are erasers, desks, houses, wires, tires, books, cloth, chairs, containers, transistors, dolls, hairpieces, ladders, envelopes, buildings, floppy disks, knives, hand tools, and boxes.

There is some overlap between the machine and the manufacture categories. Many devices, such as mechanical pencils, cigarette lighters, and electronic circuits can be classified as either.

Manufactures do not include naturally occurring things, like rocks, gold, shrimp, and wood, or slightly modified naturally occurring things, like a shrimp with its head and vein removed. However if an inventor discovers a new and unobvious use for a naturally occurring thing, such as a way to use the molecules in a piece of gold as part of a computer memory, this invention can be patented as a new use (see below), or as a machine.

4. Statutory Classes: Compositions of Matter

Compositions of matter are items such as chemical compositions, conglomerates, aggregates, or other chemically significant substances that are usually supplied in bulk (solid or particulate), liquid, or gaseous form. Examples are road-building compositions, all chemicals, gasoline, fuel gas, glue, paper, soap, drugs, microbes, food additives, drugs, and plastics.

Although naturally occurring things such as wood and rocks can't be patented, purified forms of naturally occurring things, such as medicinals extracted from herbs, can be. One inventor obtained a composi-

tion of matter patent on a new element he discovered. Recently, genetically altered plants, microbes, and nonhuman animals have been allowed under this category. Compositions sometimes overlap with manufactures. Unlike manufactures, compositions are usually similar chemical compositions or aggregates whose chemical natures are of primary importance and whose shapes are of secondary import. Manufactures are items whose physical shapes are significant, but whose chemical compositions are of lesser import.

5. Statutory Classes: New Uses of Any of the Above

A new-use invention is actually a new and nonobvious process or method for using an old and known invention. The inventive act isn't the creation of a new thing or process, but the discovery of a new use for something that is old.

An inventor who discovers a new and nonobvious use of an old invention or thing, can get a patent on the discovery. For example, suppose an inventor discovers that a venetian-blind cleaning device can also be used as a seed planter. The inventor can't get a patent on the physical hardware that constitutes the venetian-blind cleaning device, since the inventor didn't create it—someone already patented, invented, or designed it first—but an inventor can get a patent on the specific new use (seed planting). In other examples, one inventor

Examples of Inventions That Don't Fit Within a Statutory Class

- Processes performed solely with one's mind (such as a method of meditation or a method of speed-reading) which does not involve novel body actions.
- Naturally occurring phenomena and articles, even if modified somewhat.
- Laws of nature, including abstract scientific or mathematical principles. (John Napier's invention of logarithms in 1614 was immensely innovative and valuable, but today it would never get past the bottom level of the patentability steps.)
- An arrangement of printed matter without some accompanying instrumentality. Printed matter by itself isn't patentable, but a printed label on a mattress telling how to turn it to ensure even wear, or dictionary index tabs that guide a reader to the desired word more rapidly, have been patented as articles of manufacture.
- Methods or computer programs that have no practical utility, that is, that don't produce any commercially useful and tangible result. Thus, an algorithm for solving π to 15 decimal places or extracting square roots would not be in a statutory class, but securities trading systems, credit accounting systems, etc., involving account and file postings, have been held patentable.
- Ideas. Thoughts or goals not expressed in concrete form or use are not assignable to any of the five categories above. An inventor must show how an idea can be made and used in tangible form so as to be useful. Even if this expression is only on paper, the PTO will accept it.

obtained a patent on a new use for aspirin: feeding it to swine to increase their rate of growth, and one got a patent on the new use of a powerful vacuum to suck prairie dogs out of the ground.

New-use inventions are relatively rare and technically are a form of, and must be claimed as, a process. (35 U.S.C. §100(b).) However, most patent experts treat them as a distinct category.

C. Utility

To be patentable an invention must be useful. Patent applications are rarely rejected for lack of utility. Any usefulness will suffice, provided the usefulness is functional and not aesthetic. However, utility is occasionally an issue when an inventor tries to patent a new chemical for which a use hasn't yet been found but for which its inventor will likely find a use later. If the inventor can't state (and prove, if challenged) a realistic use, the PTO won't grant a patent on the chemical. A chemical that can be used to produce another useful chemical is itself regarded as useful.

Commercially sold software-based inventions almost always inherently satisfy the utility requirement, since virtually all software has a utilitarian function, even if used to create aesthetic designs on an idle monitor, compute the value of mutual funds, or evaluate golf scores.

Despite the fact that virtually all inventions are useful in the literal sense of the word, some types of inventions are deemed "not useful" as a matter of law, and patents on them are accordingly denied by the PTO. Below are some examples.

- **Unsafe New Drugs.** The PTO won't grant a patent on any new drug unless the applicant can show that not only is it useful in treating some condition, but also that it's relatively safe for its intended purpose. In other words, the PTO considers an unsafe drug useless. Most drug patent applications won't be allowed unless the Food and Drug Administration (FDA) has approved tests of the drug for efficacy and safety. Drugs that are generally recognized as safe, or are in a "safe" chemical category with known safe drugs, don't need prior FDA approval to be patentable.

- **Whimsical Inventions.** On rare occasions, the PTO will reject an applica-

tion for a patent when it finds the invention to be totally whimsical, even though "useful" in some bizarre sense. This standard is rarely applied. For example, in 1937 the PTO issued a patent on a rear windshield (with tail-operated wiper) for a horse (Pat. No. 2,079,053). The PTO regarded this as having utility as an amusement.

- **Inventions Useful Only for Illegal Purposes.** The PTO won't issue patents on inventions useful solely for illegal purposes such as disabling burglar alarms, safecracking, copying currency, and defrauding the public. However, many inventions in this category can be described or claimed in a "legal" way. For example, a police radar detector would qualify for a patent if it's described as a tester to see if a radar is working or as a device for reminding drivers to watch their speed.

- **Immoral Inventions.** In the past, the PTO has included morality in its requirements, rejecting inventions believed to be morally objectionable. In recent years, with increased sexual liberality, the requirement is now virtually nonexistent. The PTO now regularly issues patents on sexual aids and stimulants.

- **Non-Operable Inventions.** Another facet of the useful requirement is operability. The invention must appear to the PTO to be workable. The PTO will reject as non-operable an esoteric invention that looks technically questionable (in other words, it looks like it just plain won't work). If the examiner questions operability—a rare occurrence—the inventor has the burden of proving its operability. All patent examiners have technical degrees and can apply a very stringent test if the operability of an invention is questioned.

- **Nuclear Weapons.** Nuclear weapons aren't patentable because of a special statute.
- **Theoretical Phenomena.** Theoretical phenomena, such as the phenomenon of superconductivity or the transistor effect, aren't patentable.
- **Aesthetic Purpose.** If the invention's sole purpose or "function" is aesthetic, the PTO will reject it as lacking utility. These inventions should usually be the subject of a design patent application. For example, consider a computer case whose unique shape does not make the computer operate better. If the only novelty is the aesthetics of the design, the case could be covered by a design patent. If the shape of the computer case made it cheaper to manufacture, then it has utility and could be subject to a utility patent.

D. Novelty and Prior Art

In 1910, the company founded by the Wright Brothers sued a company that had infringed the rudder on its new flying machine. The company being sued argued that the flying machine's rudder was not novel because such rudders had been developed and written about before the Wright Brothers. Judge Learned Hand, a famous jurist, disagreed, noting mankind's previous difficulty in becoming airborne. "The number of persons who can fly at all is so limited that it is not surprising that infringers have not arisen in great numbers," he added wryly. The criteria for novelty has not changed dramatically since the Wright Brothers, but before examining this standard, it is necessary to review a principle known as prior art. In Chapter 4, we discuss how to search for prior art.

1. Prior Art

An invention must be novel in order to qualify for a patent. In order for an invention to meet this novelty test it must differ physically in some way from all prior developments that are available to the public anywhere in the world. In the realm of patent law, these prior developments and concepts are collectively referred to as "prior art." According to Section 102 of the patent laws, the term "prior art" means generally the state of knowledge existing or publicly available either before the date of an invention or more than one year prior to the patent application date.

a. Date of an Invention

In order to decide what prior art is with respect to any given invention, it's first necessary to determine the "date of invention." Most inventors think it's the date on which one files a patent application. However, the "date of invention" is the earliest of the following dates:

- the date an inventor filed the patent application (provisional or regular),
- the date an inventor can prove that the invention was built and tested (known as "reduction to practice"— see Reduction to Practice sidebar, below) in the U.S. or a country that is a member of North American Free Trade Association (NAFTA) or the World Trade Organization (WTO). (35 U.S.C. § 104), or
- the date an inventor can prove that the invention was conceived in a NAFTA or WTO country, provided the inventor can also prove diligence in building and testing it or filing a patent application on it. Most industrial countries are members of the WTO and a listing of WTO signatories is provided at the PTO website.

An inventor who maintains proper records (see Chapter 3) and was diligent afterwards will be able to use the date of conception, which is usually several months before the filing date. Once the date of invention is determined, the relevant "prior art" comprises everything available before that date or anything available about the invention more than one year prior to filing the application.

Reduction to Practice

Reduction to practice occurs when the inventor can demonstrate that the invention works for its intended purpose. This can be accomplished by building and testing the invention (actual reduction to practice) or by preparing a patent application or provisional patent application that shows how to make and use the invention and that it works (constructive reduction practice). In the event of a dispute or a challenge at the PTO, invention documentation is essential in proving the "how and when" of conception and reduction to practice. (For more information about invention documentation, see Chapter 3.)

b. The One-Year Rule

In addition to the six categories below, prior art includes knowledge about an invention that has become publicly known more than one year prior to the date an inventor files a regular patent application or a provisional patent application. Known as the "one-year rule," the patent laws state that an inventor must file a patent application within one year after an inventor sells, offers for sale, or commercially or publicly uses or describes an invention. If an inventor fails to file within one year of such occurrence, the inventor is barred from obtaining a patent. If the PTO is unaware of the public sale or use and issues a patent, the patent will be declared invalid if it can later be shown that the invention was publicly shown or sold.

> EXAMPLE: A 3M employee developed a method for perforating carbonless paper with a laser and arranged for the manufacture of 10,000 forms using the laser-perforated sheets. In July 1989, the laser-perforated forms were distributed throughout the company for use by thousands of 3M employees. 3M filed a patent application for its laser-perforation method in August 1990. After 3M acquired a patent, 3M sued Appleton Papers for infringement of the process. As a defense, Appleton claimed that the patent was invalid because 3M put the invention "in public use" more than one year prior to the date of its patent application. A federal court determined that the internal distribution at 3M constituted a public use and the patent was declared invalid. (*3M v. Appleton Papers Inc.*, 35 F. Supp. 2d 1138 (D. Minn. 1999).)

Foreign Filing and the One-Year Rule

While an inventor has a year after publication or use to file in the U.S., most foreign countries aren't so lenient. If an inventor intends to file a foreign patent application, the invention should not be offered for sale, sold, publicly used, or published anywhere before the inventor files in the U.S. For instance, suppose an inventor creates a new type of paint roller on 2000 November 16. If the inventor has no intention of filing in another country, the inventor can use, publish, or sell the invention immediately and still file the U.S. patent application (PPA or regular) any time up to 2001 November 16. However, any inventor who may eventually want to file a foreign application, should file in the U.S. before publicizing the invention. This way the inventor can publish or sell the invention freely without the loss of any foreign rights in the major industrial countries, provided the inventor files there within one year after the U.S. filing date. Under an international agreement, the inventor is entitled to the U.S. filing date in such countries. In countries that are not party to any patent treaties (for example, Colombia and Pakistan), the inventor must file before publicizing the invention. (For more information about foreign patents, see Chapter 9.)

Year Date Format

The year-month-day date format (2000 June 10) used in this book is from the International Standards Organization (ISO). It is commonly used in computer-speak and in trademark applications. It provides a logical descending order that facilitates calculating the one-year rule and other periods.

Computer Publications

While the statute speaks of "printed" publications, we believe that information which is publicly accessible on a computer-information utilities or network would be considered a printed publication.

---

c. Specifics of Prior Art

Now we'll take a closer look at the definition of prior art. (35 U.S.C. §102.)

i. Prior Printed Publications Anywhere

Prior art, meaning any printed publication, written by anyone, and from anywhere in the world, in any language, will be considered if it was published either:

a. before the earliest provable date of invention (see above), or

b. over one year before an inventor files a patent application.

The term "printed publication" is very loosely interpreted and the PTO has even used old Dick Tracy comic strips showing a wristwatch radio as prior art. Generally, printed publications include patents (U.S. and foreign), books, magazines (including trade and professional journals), publicly available technical papers and abstracts, and even photocopied theses, provided they were made publicly available by putting them in a college library.

The "prior printed publications" category is the most important category of prior art and will generally constitute most of the prior art encountered. Most of the prior printed publications that the PTO refers to when it's processing an application will be U.S. patents.

ii. U.S. Patents Filed by Others Prior to the Invention's Conception

Any U.S. patent that has a filing date earlier than an inventor's earliest provable date of invention is considered valid prior art. This is so even if the patent issues after an inventor files an application. For example, suppose an inventor named Jones conceives of an invention on 2001 June 9 and files a patent application on 2001 August 9, two months later. Six months after Jones's filing date, on 2002 February 9, a patent to another inventor named Goldberger issues that shows all or part of Jones' invention. If Goldberger's patent was any other type of publication, it wouldn't be prior art to Jones's application since it was published after Jones's filing date. However if Goldberger's patent application was filed on 2002 June 8, one day earlier than Jones's date of conception, the PTO must consider the Goldberger patent as prior art to the Jones application. (35 U.S.C. §102(e).)

It is a common misconception that only in-force patents (that is, patents that haven't yet expired) count as prior art. Any earlier patent, even if it was issued 150 years ago, will constitute prior art against an invention. (For information about how to search for patents, see Chapter 4.)

iii. Publicly Available Knowledge or Use of the Invention in the U.S.

Prior art is valid even if there's no written record of it. Any public knowledge of the invention will constitute valid prior art. Likewise, use of the invention by the inventor (or others in the U.S.) before the inventor's earliest provable date of invention, or one year before the inventor files a patent application, will constitute valid prior art. For example, an earlier heat-treating process used openly by a blacksmith in a small town, although never published or widely known, is a prior public use that will defeat an inventor's right to a patent on a similar process. It has been held that allowing even one person to use an invention without restriction will constitute public use. With respect to public knowledge, an example would be a talk at a publicly accessible technical society. Recently, even a showing of a kaleidoscope without restriction at a party with 30 attendees was held to be prior public knowledge.

For still another example of a public use, suppose that an inventor invented a new type of paint and uses it to paint his building in downtown Philadelphia. The inventor forgets to file a patent application and leaves the paint on for 13 months. It's now too late to file a valid patent application since the invention was used publicly for over a year.

This public-use-and-knowledge category of prior art is almost never used by the PTO because they have no way of uncovering it. The PTO searches only patents and other publications. Occasionally, however, if defendants (infringers) in patent lawsuits happen to uncover a prior public use, they can then rely on it to invalidate the patent and escape liability for infringement.

Experimental Exception

If a prior public use was for bona fide (good faith) experimental purposes, it doesn't count as prior art. For example, suppose in the "painted Philadelphia building" example above, that an inventor painted his building to test the durability of the new paint: Each month the inventor photographed it, kept records on its reflectivity, wear resistance, and adhesion. In this case the one-year period wouldn't begin to run until the bona fide experimentation stopped.

iv. An Inventor's Prior Foreign Patents

If an inventor (or the inventor's legal representative) obtains any foreign patent before the inventor's U.S. filing date and the foreign patent application was filed over a year before the U.S. filing date, it is valid prior art. This category is generally pertinent to non-U.S. residents who start the patenting process in a foreign country. An inventor in this class must file the U.S. application either within one year after filing in the foreign country or before the foreign patent issues. However, an inventor seeking the benefit of a foreign filing date for a U.S. application should file in the U.S. within the one year after the foreign filing date. (For more information about foreign patents, see Chapter 9.)

v. Prior U.S. Inventor

If someone (the first inventor) in the U.S. invented substantially the same invention before the date of conception of another inventor (the second inventor), then the first inventor's invention (even though no written record was made) can be used to defeat a right to a patent for the second inventor.

However, under a new statute, if an invention is novel and the first inventor worked in the same organization as the second inventor, then the first inventor's work won't be considered prior art. When two or more inventors each file a patent application on the same invention, the PTO will declare an "interference" between the two competing applications. (For more on interferences, see Chapter 6, Section C.) The winner of the interference will be the first inventor to reduce the invention to practice, unless the other inventor conceived of it first and was diligent in reducing it to practice.

vi. Prior Sale or On-Sale Status in the U.S.

The law also considers certain actions by humans to be "prior art," even when no paper records exist. These actions involve the "sale" or "on-sale" category. Suppose an inventor offers to sell, sells, or commercially uses an invention in the U.S. The inventor must file the U.S. patent application within one year after this offer, sale, or commercial use. This is another part of the "one-year rule." This means that if an inventor makes sales to test the commercial feasibility, the inventor has a year after the first sale to file in the U.S. Again, however, any sale before filing will defeat the inventor's right to a patent in most foreign countries. (See Chapter 9 for rules on foreign filing.)

In order to start the one-year period running, the sale or offer of sale must be a commercial offer to sell or a sale of actual hardware or a process embodying the invention. This is true even if the invention has not yet been built, so long as it has been drawn or described in reasonable detail. However, an offer to license or sell, or an actual sale of the inventive concept (not hardware) to a manufacturer, will not start the one-year period running.

Abandonment

If an inventor "abandons" an invention by finally giving up on it in some way, and this comes to the attention of the PTO or any court charged with ruling on the patent, the application or patent will be rejected or ruled invalid.

EXAMPLE: An inventor made a model of an invention, tested it, failed to get it to work or failed to sell it, and then consciously dropped all efforts on it. Later the inventor changes her mind and tries to patent it. If the abandonment becomes known, the inventor would lose the right to a patent. But if the inventor merely stops work on it for a number of years because of such reasons as health, finances, or lack of a crucial part, but intends to pursue it again when possible, the law would excuse the inaction and hold that the inventor didn't abandon.

d. Summary of Prior Art

In summary, relevant prior art usually consists of:

- any published writing (including any patent) that was made publicly available either (1) before the earliest provable date of the invention, or

(2) over one year before an inventor can get the patent application on file
- any U.S. patent whose issue date isn't early enough to stop an inventor but that has a filing date earlier than the earliest provable date of invention
- any relevant invention or development (whether described in writing or not) existing prior to when an invention was conceived, or
- any public or commercial use, sale, or knowledge of the invention more than one year prior to an application filing date.

2. Any Physical Difference Will Satisfy the Novelty Requirement

The law generally recognizes three types of novelty, any one of which will satisfy the novelty requirement of Section 102: (1) physical (hardware or method) difference, (2) new combination, and (3) new use.

a. Physical Differences

This is the most common way to satisfy the novelty requirement. Here an invention has some physical or structural (hardware or method) difference over the prior art. If the invention is a machine, composition, or article, it must be or have one or more parts that have a different shape, value, size, color, or composition than what's already known.

It's often difficult for inventors to distinguish between a physical difference and a new result. When asked, "What's physically different about the invention?" inventors often reply that it is lighter, faster, safer, cheaper to make or use, or portable. However, these factors are new results or advantages, not physical differences, and are primarily relevant to nonobviousness (see Section E) not to novelty. A new physical feature must be a difference in the hardware.

Even omitting an element can be considered novel. For example, if a machine has always had four gears, and an inventor finds that it will work with three, the novelty requirement is satisfied.

Also, the discovery of a critical area of a given prior art range will be considered novel. That is, if a prior art magazine article on fabric dyeing states that a substance will work at a temperature range of 100–150 degrees centigrade and an inventor discovers that it works five times better at 127–130 degrees centigrade, the law will still consider this range novel even though it's technically embraced by the prior art.

One area of novelty which is frequently overlooked is the new arrangement: If an inventor comes up with a new arrangement of an old combination of elements, the new arrangement will satisfy the novelty requirement. For example, see the new combination in Section 2b below, where the arrangement, not its combination, is novel.

A physical difference can also be subtle or less apparent in the hardware sense, so that it's manifested primarily by a different mode of operation. For example, an electronic amplifying circuit that looks the same, but that operates in a different mode—say Class A rather than Class B—or is under the control of different software, or a pump that looks the same, but that operates at a higher pressure and hence in a different mode, will be considered novel.

Processes Note

If an invention is a new process, novel hardware is not necessary; the physical novelty is basically the new way of manipulating old hardware. Any novel step or steps will satisfy the physical novelty requirement.

b. New Combinations

Many laypersons believe that if an invention consists entirely of old components, it can't be patented. This is not true and, in fact, most inventions are made of old components. If an invention is a new combination of two old features, the PTO will consider it novel. For a combination invention to be considered as lacking novelty, all of its physical characteristics must exist in a single prior art reference. For example, suppose an inventor "invents" a bicycle made of one of the recently discovered, superstrength, carbon-fiber alloys. The bicycle would clearly be considered novel since it has a new physical feature: a frame that is made, for the first time, of a carbon-fiber alloy. But, remember, just because it's novel, useful, and fits within a statutory class, doesn't mean the bicycle is patentable. It still must pass the test of nonobviousness (see Section E).

c. New Use

If you've invented a new use for an old item of hardware or an old process, the new use will satisfy the novelty requirement no matter how trivial the "newness." For example, Dorie invents a new vegetable cooker which, after a search, she discovers is exactly like a copper smelter invented by one Jaschik in 1830. Doric's cooker, even though identical to Jaschik's smelter, will be considered novel since it's for a different use. However, if an invention involves novel physical hardware, technically it can't be a new-use invention.

E. Nonobviousness

In this section we explore the most important (and most misunderstood) legal requirement for obtaining a patent: whether an invention is nonobvious. Even though an invention is physically different from the prior art, this isn't enough to qualify for a patent. To obtain a patent, the differences must be significant. The legal term for such a difference is "unobvious" or, commonly, "nonobvious." In order to obtain a patent, the differences between the invention and the prior art must not be obvious to one with ordinary skill in the field. Or as it is sometimes put, the invention must provide one or more new and unexpected results.

In the following sections, we discuss examples of "nonobviousness" and "obviousness." We also cover the types of arguments based on external circumstances (called "secondary factors") that are often made to bolster an inventor's contention that an invention is unobvious. A patentability flowchart is provided below as Figure 2B to help you understand the slippery concept of nonobviousness and the role it plays in the patent application process. In addition to presenting all of the criteria used by the PTO and the courts for determining whether an invention is nonobvious, the chart also incorporates the first three tests of statutory class, usefulness, and novelty.

1. How Patent Examiners Determine "Nonobviousness"

Just how do patent examiners determine whether or not an invention is obvious? Patent examiners first make a search and gather all of the patents and other prior art that they feel are relevant or close to the invention for which a patent is sought. Then they examine these patents and any prior-art references provided with the patent application and see whether the invention contains any novel physical features, new combinations, or new uses that aren't shown in any reference. If so, an invention is novel. (Novelty is discussed in Section D.)

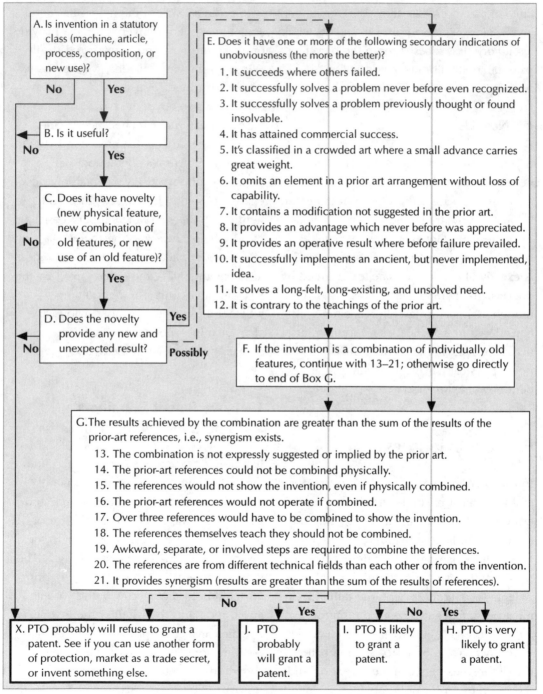

Figure 2B—The Patentability Flowchart

Next they see whether the novelty produces any unexpected or surprising results. If so, they'll find that the invention is nonobvious and grant an inventor a patent. If not (this usually occurs the first time they act on a case), they'll reject the application (sometimes termed a "shotgun" or "shoot-from-the-hip" rejection) and leave it to an inventor to show that the new features do indeed produce new and unexpected results. To do this, an inventor may use many of the relevant reasons listed in this chapter. If an inventor can convince the examiner, the inventor will get the patent.

If a dispute over nonobviousness actually finds its way into court, however, both sides will present the testimony of patent lawyers or technical experts who fit, or most closely fit, the hypothetical job descriptions called for by the particular case. These experts will testify for or against obviousness by arguing that the invention does or doesn't produce new and unexpected results.

2. Nonobvious to Whom?

It doesn't tell anyone much to say an invention must be nonobvious. The big question is, nonobvious to whom? A patent will not be issued if a person having ordinary skill in the field of the invention would consider the invention obvious at the time of creation.

The law considers a person having ordinary skill in the art to be a worker in the field of the invention who has (1) ordinary skill, but who (2) is totally knowledgeable

about all the prior art in his or her field. This is a pure fantasy since no such person ever lived, or ever will, but there's no other realistic way to approach an objective standard for determining nonobviousness. Instead, the PTO creates a hypothetical person and tries to weigh the obviousness of the invention against the knowledge this hypothetical person would possess.

Consider some examples. Assume that an invention has to do with electronics—say a new computer circuit process. A typical computer circuit design engineer with total knowledge of all computer circuits would be an imaginary skilled artisan. If an invention is mechanical, such as an improved cigarette lighter or belt buckle, the PTO would try to postulate a hypothetical cigarette-lighter engineer or belt-buckle designer with ordinary skill and comprehensive knowledge.

3. What Does "Obvious" Mean?

So many commonplace inventions, such as bifocals and paper clips, seem obvious to us now, but were actually quite revolutionary in their time. Over the years, many tests for nonobviousness have been used by the courts. One important decision stated that nonobviousness is manifested if the invention produces "unusual and surprising results." The U.S. Supreme Court, which has final say in such matters, decreed the steps for determining nonobviousness in the case of *Graham v. John Deere*. These are the steps:

1. Determine the scope and content of the prior art.
2. Determine the novelty of the invention.
3. Determine the level of skill of artisans in the pertinent art.
4. Against this background, determine the obviousness or nonobviousness of the inventive subject matter.
5. Also consider secondary and objective factors such as commercial success, long-felt but unsolved need, and failure of others. (*Graham v. John Deere*, 383 U.S. 1 (1966).)

Unfortunately, the Supreme Court's decision added nothing to the understanding of the terms "obviousness" and "nonobviousness." In the crucial step (#4), the court merely repeated the very terms (obvious and nonobvious) it was seeking to define. Therefore, most attorneys and patent examiners continue to look for new and unexpected results that flow from the novel features when seeking to determine if an invention is obvious.

Despite its failure to define the term obvious, the Supreme Court did add an important step to the process by which obviousness is to be determined. In Step #5, the court made clear that objective circumstances must be taken into account by the PTO or courts when deciding whether an invention is or isn't obvious. The court specifically mentioned three such circumstances: commercial success, long-felt but unsolved need, and failure of others to come up with the invention.

Although an invention might not, strictly speaking, produce "new and unexpected results" from the standpoint of one with "ordinary skill in the art," it still may be considered nonobvious if it can be shown that the invention has met some of these secondary factors (described in more detail in Section E5.)

4. Examples of Obviousness and Nonobviousness

In the following sections we describe circumstances that can affect a determination of nonobviousness.

a. Nonobvious: Slight Physical Changes—Dramatic Result

Usually an invention must demonstrate a significant physical change to be considered nonobvious. However, on some occasions, a very slight change in the shape, slope, size, or material can produce a patentable invention that operates entirely differently and produces totally unexpected results.

EXAMPLE: Consider the original centrifugal vegetable juicer composed of a spinning perforated basket with a vertical sidewall and a nonperforated grater bottom. When vegetables, such as carrots, were pushed into the grater bottom, they were grated into fine pieces and juice that were thrown against the sidewall of the basket. The juice passed through the perforations and was recovered in a container, but the pieces clung to the sidewalls, adding weight to the basket and closing the perforations, making the machine impossible to run and operate after a relatively small amount of vegetables were juiced. Then someone discovered that making the side of the basket slope outward still allowed for juice extraction through the perforated side of the basket, but now the pulp, instead of adhering to the old vertical side of the basket, was centrifugally forced up the new sloped side of the basket where it would go over the top and be diverted to a separate receptacle. Thus the juicer could be operated continuously without the pulp having to be cleaned out. Obviously, despite the fact that the physical novelty was slight and involved merely changing the slope of a basket's sidewall, the result was entirely new and unexpected. It was therefore considered nonobvious.

b. Nonobvious: New Use Inventions

New-use inventions don't involve any physical change at all in the old invention. However, in order to be considered nonobvious, the new use must be (1) a different use of some known product or process, and (2) the different use must produce new, unexpected results.

EXAMPLE: An inventor determined that feeding aspirin to swine increased their rate of growth. This discovery was considered nonobvious because the result—faster growing swine—was unexpected since it wasn't described or suggested in the prior art.

c. Obvious: Different Element, Similar Function

The courts have held that the substitution of a different, but similarly functioning, element for one of the elements in a known combination, although creating a "novel" invention, won't produce a nonobvious one. For example, many companies in the 1950s substituted transistors for vacuum tubes in amplifier circuits. This new combination of old elements provided tremendous new results (decreased power consumption, size, heat, weight, and far greater longevity), but it wasn't patentable because the results were foreseeable. The power reduction and reduced-weight advantages of transistors would have been already known as soon as a transistor made its appearance. Thus, substituting them for tubes wouldn't provide the old amplifier circuit with any unexpected new results. Accordingly, the PTO's Board of Appeals held the new combination to be obvious to an artisan of ordinary skill at the time.

d. Obvious: Old Concept, New Form

The PTO will also consider as obvious the mere carrying forward of an old concept, or a change in form and degree, without a new result. For instance, when one inventor provided notches on the inner rim of a steering wheel to provide a better grip, the idea was held to be obvious because of medieval sword handles that had similar notches for the same purpose. And the use of a large pulley for a logging rig was held nonpatentable over the use of a small pulley for clotheslines. These cases are known as "obviousness by analogy."

> **EXAMPLE:** Lou comes up with a way to make mustard-flavored hot dog buns— mix powdered mustard with the flour. Even though Lou's recipe is novel, the PTO will almost certainly hold it to be obvious since the result of the new combination is entirely foreseeable and expected.

There is an exception to this rule. If the substitution provides unexpected new results, the law will hold it nonobvious.

e. Obvious: Duplication of Parts

The courts and the PTO will usually consider the duplication of a part as obvious unless new results can be observed. For instance, in an automobile, the substitution of two banks of three cylinders with two carburetors was held obvious over a six-cylinder, single-carburetor engine, since the new arrangement had no unexpected advantages. However, there are exceptions to this rule. For example, the use of two water turbines to provide cross flow to eliminate axial thrust on bearings was held nonobvious over a single turbine; again, an unexpected, new result.

f. Obvious: Portability, Size, Speed, and Integration

Making devices portable, making parts smaller or larger, faster or slower, effecting a substitution of equivalents (a roller bearing for a ball bearing), making elements adjustable, making parts integral, separable (modular), or in kit form, and other known techniques with their known advantages, will be held obvious unless new, unexpected results can be shown.

5. Secondary Factors in Determining Nonobviousness

As mentioned, if the new and unexpected results of an invention are marginal, an inventor may still be able to get a patent if an inventor can show that an invention possesses one or more secondary factors that establish nonobviousness. While the Supreme Court listed only three in the *John Deere* case, we have compiled a list of factors that the PTO and the courts consider.

These secondary factors must generally only be dealt with if the PTO makes a preliminary finding of obviousness or if an invention is attacked in court as being obvious. Although some of these secondary factors may appear similar, consider each independently, since the courts have recognized subtle differences.

- **Previous Failure of Others.** If the invention is successful where previous workers in the field were unable to make it work, this will be of great help to the application. For instance, many previous attempts were made to use electrostatic methods for making photocopies, but all failed. Chester Carlson (a patent attorney himself) came along and successfully used an electrostatic process to make copies. This greatly enhanced his case for the patentability of his dry (xerographic) photocopying process.

- **Solves an Unrecognized Problem.** Some inventions solve problems that are not obvious. Consider a showerhead that automatically shuts off in case of extreme water temperature. As the problem was probably never recognized in the prior art, the solution would therefore probably be non-obvious.

- **Solves an Insoluble Problem.** Suppose that for years those skilled in the art had tried and failed to solve a problem and the art and literature were full of unsuccessful "solutions." Nonobviousness may be demonstrated if an inventor finds a workable solution, for example a cure for the common cold.

- **Commercial Success.** If an invention has attained commercial success, this helps to prove nonobviousness. After all, nothing succeeds like success, right? However, this argument is not always available because many inventors don't sell the invention before the application is filed, either because of concern over foreign patent rights or the one-year rule.

- **Crowded Art.** If an invention is in a crowded field of invention—for example, a field that is mature and that contains many patents, such as electrical connectors or bicycles—a small advance will go farther towards qualifying the invention for a patent than it will in a new, blossoming field of invention.

- **Omission of Element.** If an inventor can omit an element in a prior invention without loss of capability, this will count a lot towards proving nonobviousness since parts are often expensive, unreliable, heavy, and labor-intensive.

- **Unsuggested Modification.** If an inventor can modify a prior invention in a manner not suggested before, such as by increasing the slope in a paper-making machine, or by making the basket slope in a centrifugal juice extractor, this act in itself counts for nonobviousness.

- **Unappreciated Advantage.** If an invention provides an advantage that was never before appreciated, it can make a difference. In a recent case, a gas cap that was impossible to insert in a skewed manner was held to be patentable since it provided an advantage that was never previously appreciated.

- **Solves Prior Inoperability.** If an invention provides an operative result where before only inoperability existed, then it has a good chance for a patent. For instance, nonobviousness would be proved if an inventor came up with a gasoline additive that prevented huge fires in case of a plane crash, since all previous fire-suppressant additives had been largely unsuccessful.

- **Successful Implementation of Ancient Idea.** Consider the Wright Brothers' airplane. For centuries humans had wanted to fly and had tried many unsuccessful schemes. The successful implementation of such an ancient desire carries great weight when it comes to proving nonobviousness.

- **Solution of Long-Felt Need.** Suppose an inventor finds a way to prevent tailgate-type automobile crashes. This solves a powerful need and the solution will help demonstrate nonobviousness.

- **Contrary to Prior Art's Teaching.** If the prior art expressly teaches that something can't be done or is impractical—for example, humans can't fly without artificial propulsion motors—a patent will issue if the inventor can prove this teaching wrong.

6. Combination Inventions: Secondary Factors

Inventions that combine two or more elements already known in the prior art can still be patentable, provided the combination can be considered nonobvious—that is, it's a new combination and it produces new and unexpected results. In fact, most patents are granted on such combinations since very few truly new things are ever discovered. Below are some of the factors used to determine the nonobviousness of "combination inventions" (that is, inventions that have two or more features that are shown in two or more prior-art references).

- **Synergism (2 + 2 = 5).** If the results achieved by a combination invention are greater than the sum of the separate results of its parts, this can indicate nonobviousness. Consider a pistol trigger release where a magnetic ring must be worn to fire the pistol. The results (increased police safety) are far in excess of what magnets, rings, and pistols could provide separately.

- **Combination Unsuggested.** If the prior art contains no suggestion, either expressed or implied, that the references should be combined, this weighs in favor of nonobviousness.

- **Impossible to Combine.** If the prior-art references show the separate elements of the inventive combination, but in a way that makes it seem they would be physically impossible to combine, this can demonstrate nonobviousness.

- **Different Combination.** An inventor has a good case for nonobviousness if the prior art for the combination of elements shows a different, albeit possibly confusingly similar, combination to the result obtained by the inventor.
- **Prior-Art References Would Not Operate in Combination.** An inventor also has a good case for nonobviousness if prior-art references indicate that the combination of elements wouldn't operate properly, for example, due to some incompatibility. If an inventor found a way to make that combination work, this would favor nonobviousness.
- **References From a Different Field.** If the prior-art references show structures that are similar to an invention, but are in a different technical field, this helps demonstrate nonobviousness.

There are additional arguments that can be made to demonstrate nonobviousness, much of which are beyond the scope of this book. For additional information, review some of the patent resources provided in the Chapter 10, Help Beyond This Book..

F. Legal Requirements for a Design Patent

To be patentable, the appearance of a design, as a whole, must be novel (different from previous designs) and nonobvious to a designer of ordinary skill. The design must be purely ornamental, not functional. As one judge stated, the design must be created for the purpose of "ornamenting" a functional object. For example, many utilitarian articles are pleasing to look at, such as a ball bearing or a Frisbee. But in these cases, the design is dictated by the function. These designs do not add ornamentation.

To be patentable, the design must be visible during normal intended use or at some other commercially important time. This requirement can be satisfied if the design is visible at the time of sale or in an advertisement. For example, the design of a hip prosthesis may not be visible when in use, but it is visible at the time of purchase and in advertisements.

G. Legal Requirements for a Plant Patent

Two types of patents are issued for plants: plant patents and utility patents.

1. Plant Patents

Since 1930, the U.S. has been granting plant patents under the Plant Patent Act to any person who first appreciates the distinctive qualities of a plant and reproduces it asexually. Asexual reproduction means reproducing the plant by a means other than seeds, usually by grafting or cloning the plant tissue. If it cannot be duplicated by asexual reproduction, it cannot be the subject of a plant patent. In addition, the patented plant must also be novel and distinctive. Generally, this means that the plant must have at least one significant distinguishing characteristic to establish it as a distinct variety. For example, a rose may be novel and distinctive if it is nearly thornless and has a unique two-tone color scheme. Tuber-propagated plants (such as potatoes) and plants found in an uncultivated state cannot receive a plant patent. (35 U.S.C. §§161-164.)

There is a limit on the extent of plant patent rights. Generally, a plant patent can only be infringed when a plant has been asexually reproduced from the actual plant protected by the plant patent. In other words, the infringing plant must have more than similar characteristics—it must have the same genetics as the patented plant

2. Utility Patents for Plants

Since the late 1980s, utility patents have been issued for man-made plants or elements of plants. These plants can be reproduced either sexually (by seeds) or asexually. These patents have been issued for elements of plants such as proteins, genes, DNA, buds, pollen, fruit, plant-based chemicals, and the processes used in the manufacture of these plant products. To obtain a utility patent, the plant must be made by humans and must fit within the statutory requirements (utility, novelty, and nonobviousness). The patent must describe and claim the specific characteristics of the plant for which protection is sought. Sometimes the best way to meet this requirement is to deposit seeds or plant tissue at a specified public depository. For example, many countries have International Depository Authorities for such purposes.

Although a utility patent is harder and more time consuming to acquire than a plant patent, a utility patent is considered to be a stronger form of protection. For example, a plant protected by a utility patent can be infringed if it is reproduced either sexually or asexually. Since the utility patent owner can prevent others from making and using the invention, does this mean the buyer of a patented seed cannot sell the resulting plants to the public? No, under patent laws, the purchaser can sell the plants but cannot manufacture the seed line. ■

Invention Documentation

Years after obtaining a patent on the telephone, Alexander Graham Bell was challenged by another inventor who claimed he had first devised the telephone. Bell fought a contentious lawsuit and proved, with the aid of his lab documents and his wife's testimony, that his invention had priority. Patent protection is often dependent on proving how and when someone conceived of and built an invention. In this chapter, we discuss documentation of inventions, an essential element in the patent process because it authenticates the invention process.

A. The Importance of Documentation

Documentation is the process by which the inventor records the dates and events related to the conception and building of an invention. Documenting the development of an invention is important for the following reasons:

1. Proof of Conception and Reduction to Practice

Documentation is important for proving the two foundations of patent rights: conception and reduction to practice. Conception is the mental part of inventing, how an invention is formulated or how a problem is solved. Reduction to practice means that the inventor can demonstrate that the invention works for its intended purpose. Reduction to practice can be accomplished by building and testing the invention (actual reduction to practice) or by preparing a patent application or provisional patent application that shows how to make and use the invention and that it works (constructive reduction practice). In the event of a dispute or a challenge at the PTO, these forms of documentation aid in proving the "how and when" of conception and reduction to practice.

2. Ownership Rights

Documentation establishes who is the first and true inventor and prevents confusion over ownership rights. Documentation assists in proving ownership, for example, when two inventors simultaneously and independently conceive of an invention, or when several people are working on the same problem together. If an inventor has not filed a patent application for an invention prior to starting employment, documentation assists in proving ownership of the invention should a dispute arise with the employer.

3. Defeat of Prior-Art References

A prior-art reference is any patent, other publication, or prior public knowledge or use that casts doubt on the originality of an invention. A prior-art reference has an effective date—this is usually its publication date, but if it is a U.S. patent, it's the filing date. An inventor can prevent a patent examiner from using a prior-art reference against a patent application if the inventor has documentation that shows either that:

- the inventor built and tested the invention or filed a PPA (see Section E) prior to the reference's effective date, or
- the inventor conceived of the invention prior to the reference's effective date and was diligent in building and testing the invention or filing a PPA or regular patent application up through the reference's effective date. The application must be filed within a year after the date of any publication or the issue date of any patent (see Section E).

Supporting Tax Deductions

Once an inventor spends money on an invention, the IRS considers the inventor "in business," thus enabling the deduction of all invention-related expenditures from ordinary income received. If the inventor is audited, the IRS is more inclined to allow these deductions if the inventor can support them with clear and accurate documentation records of all invention activities, including conception, building and testing, and expenditures for materials such as tools.

B. Lab Notebook

The most reliable and useful way to document an invention is to use a permanently bound notebook with the pages consecutively numbered, usually known as a lab notebook. Engineering and laboratory supply stores sell these notebooks with lines at the bottom of each page for signatures and signature dates of the inventor and the witnesses. A standard crackle-finish school notebook is also suitable, provided that the inventor numbers all of the pages consecutively, and has each page or each invention description dated, signed, and witnessed.

The lab notebook usually includes:

- descriptions of the invention and novel features
- procedures used in the building and testing of the invention
- drawings, photos, or sketches of the invention
- test results and conclusions
- discussions of any known prior-art references, and
- additional documentation, such as correspondence and purchase receipts.

The Inventor's Notebook, by Fred Grissom and David Pressman (Nolo), provides organized guidance for properly documenting the inventor's invention. More information about *The Inventor's Notebook* and how to order it can be found at the end of this book. Lab notebooks can be purchased through Eureka Lab Book, Inc. (www.eurekalabbook.com/) or Scientific Notebook Company (www.snco.com).

1. How Information Is Entered in the Notebook

Entries must be handwritten and must accurately describe how events occurred. All entries must be dated as of the date the entry is made or must include an explanation for any delays in making an entry. The inventor must sign every entry. Computer printouts or other items that can't be entered directly in the notebook can be signed, dated, and witnessed, and then pasted or affixed in the notebook in chronological order. Photos or other entries that can't be signed are pasted in the notebook with a permanent adhesive and referenced by legends using descriptive words, such as "photo taken of machine in operation," made directly in the notebook. Draw in lead lines that extend from the notebook page over onto the photo to prevent a charge of substituting subsequently made photos. These pages are signed, dated, and witnessed in the usual manner. An item covering an entire page should be referred to on an adjacent page. A sketch drawn in pencil should be photocopied and affixed in the inventor's notebook in order to preserve a permanent copy.

2. Witnessing the Notebook

Notebook entries should be witnessed because an inventor's own testimony, even if supported by a properly completed notebook, will often be inadequate for proving an entry date.

The witnesses do more than verify the inventor's signature, they actually read or view and understand the technical subject material in the notebook, including the actual tests if they are witnessing the building and testing. For this reason, the chosen witnesses should have the ability or background to understand the invention. If the invention is a very simple mechanical device, practically anyone will have the technical qualifications to be a witness. But if it involves advanced chemical or electronic concepts, a witness must possess adequate background in the field. If called upon later, the witnesses must be able to testify to their own knowledge that the facts of the entry are correct.

While one witness may be sufficient, two are preferred because this enhances the likelihood of at least one of them being available to testify at a later date. If both are available, the inventor's case will be very strong.

Some notebooks already contain a line for the inventor's signature and date on each page, together with the words "Witnessed and Understood" with lines for two signatures and dates. If the inventor's notebook doesn't already contain these

27

TITLE: Self-Adjusting Can Opener — Building & Testing

REFERENCE: Conception recorded on page 23.

DESCRIPTION: A working model of this opener was made for me by Fred Smith of Model Makers, Inc., starting Sept. 1. It was finished Sept. 13. It was made of cold-rolled steel, 13 mm. thick, with brass bearings [etc.]...

Here is the photo we took on Sept. 15:

Locking groove ——— PHOTO ——— Sliding clamp

RAMIFICATIONS: We also tried a nylon hinge, but it did not work because...

TEST DESCRIPTION: We tried the opener on fifty different cans, from size __ to size __ ...

TEST RESULTS: For the size __ cans, the opener worked as well as the Ajax brand, opening each can in an average time of 8.3 seconds, the same as we obtained with the Ajax brand. [etc.]...

INVENTOR: DATED:

Irma Inventor   0X/8/27

THE ABOVE CONFIDENTIAL INFORMATION IS WITNESSED AND UNDERSTOOD:

Steve Elias   0x/9/27

Fred Friendly   0X/9/27

Figure 3A—Sample Notebook Page

words and signature lines, the inventor should write them in.

To preserve the trade secret status of the inventor's invention, the inventor should add the words "The above confidential information is" just before the words "Witnessed and Understood." For more on trade secrecy considerations, see Section F. An inventor who does not wish to rely on witnesses can still document conception (see Section D) or reduction to practice (see Section E), by filing documents with the PTO.

C. Invention Disclosure

As an alternative to a lab notebook, an inventor can record conception, building, and testing on one or more sheets of paper in a form known as an "Invention Disclosure." (See Fig. 3B, below.) The inventor describes the invention including its title, purpose, advantages, novel features, and construction. If it has been built and tested, the results are recorded. The description of the invention is signed and dated by the inventor and preferably by two witnesses using the same standards as described in Section D. If an inventor conceives of an invention on one date, and builds and tests the invention later, the inventor should make two separate invention disclosures.

D. Documenting Conception: Disclosure Document Program (DDP)

An inventor, particularly one who does not use a lab notebook or wish to rely on witnesses, can document the conception of an invention by filing a signed document under the PTO's Disclosure Document Program (DDP). The primary advantage of the DDP is that an inventor doesn't need witnesses to provide credible evidence of the date of conception. The disadvantage is that if an inventor files a disclosure document and does nothing else, the PTO will destroy it after two years. Therefore, an inventor who plans to file a patent application based on the disclosure must do so within two years of filing. For this reason, some patent experts prefer to document conception using a lab notebook instead of the DDP. Even if the inventor uses the DDP, the inventor should still use a lab notebook to document the building and testing of an invention.

To file a DDP, the inventor sends the signed document, a cover letter, a check for the fee (currently $10), and a stamped return receipt postcard. The procedures and form for filing a disclosure document is provided in David Pressman's *Patent It Yourself* (Nolo).

Invention Disclosure

Sheet __1__ of __1__

Inventor(s): ____Irma Inventor____

Address(es): ____1919 Chestnut St., Philadelphia, PA 19103____

Title of Invention: __Self-Adjusting Can Opener__

To record **Conception**, describe: 1. Circumstances of conception, 2. Purposes and advantages of invention, 3. Description, 4. Sketches, 5. Operation, 6. Ramifications, 7. Possible novel features, and 8. Closest known prior art. To record **Building and Testing**, describe: 1. Any previous disclosure of conception, 2. Construction, 3. Ramifications, 4. Operation and Tests, and 5. Test results. Include sketches and photos, where possible. Continue on additional identical copies of this sheet if necessary; inventors and witnesses should sign all sheets.

1. I thought of this can opener while at my friend Roberta's wedding last Sunday. I saw the caterer having trouble opening small and large cans with several openers. Thinking there was a better way, I recalled my Majestic KY3 sewing machine clamp and how it was adjustable and thought to modify the left arm to accommodate a can opener head.

2. My can opener will work with all sizes of cans and is actually cheaper than the most common existing one, the UR4 made by Ideal Co. of Racine, WI.

3. My can opener comprises a sliding clamp 10, a pincer groove 12, [etc.] as shown in the following sketch:

4. Sketch:

5. Instead of sliding clamp 10, I can use a special notch as follows:

6. I believe that the combination of sliding clamp 10 and pincer groove 12 is a new one for can openers. Also I believe that it may be novel to provide a frammis head with my whatsit.

7. The Acme KZ122 can opener, mfgd. by Acme Kitchenwares of Berkeley, CA, and p. 417 of "Kitchen Tools & Their Uses" (Ready Publishers, Phila. 1981) show the closest can openers to my invention, in addition to the devices already mentioned.

Inventor(s): __Irma Inventor__   Date: __200X, Jul, 6__

_____   Date: ____ / ___ / ___

The above confidential information is Witnessed and Understood:

____Griselda Hammelfarb____   Date: __200X, Jul, 7__

____Neonore Zimla____   Date: __200X, Jul, 10__

Figure 3B—Invention Disclosure

⚠ **Beware of Patent Rip-Offs.** The DDP is often used as the basis for invention scams in which disreputable organizations prey on inventors. Their ads may describe a "special government program" whereby the Patent Office will record and preserve any invention for a nominal fee. The organization charges several hundred dollars to file a disclosure document, a procedure that the inventor could manage for $10. Despite what these scams claim, the DDP does not "secure priority," "reserve rights," or take advantage of a "grace period" for two years.

The "Post Office Patent"

There's a myth that an inventor can document conception by mailing a description of the invention to him or herself by certified (or registered) mail and keeping the sealed envelope. The PTO's Board of Appeals and Patent Interferences has ruled that such "Post Office Patents" have little legal value.

E. Documenting Reduction to Practice: Provisional Patent Application

Before 1995, there were two ways to document reduction to practice: using a lab notebook to record the building and testing of the invention, or filing a patent application. On June 8, 1995, a new system went into effect that permits an inventor to file a Provisional Patent Application (PPA), an interim document that is equivalent to a reduction to practice. If a regular patent application is filed within one year of filing the PPA, the inventor can use the PPA's filing date for the purpose of deciding whether a reference is prior-art and, in the event an interference exists, who is entitled to the patent. The PPA is not available for design patents.

The PPA must contain a description of the invention and drawings, if necessary to understand the description. The description of the invention must clearly explain how to make and use the invention. If there are several versions or modes of operation for the invention, the best mode or version must be disclosed. If the inventor wishes, claims, formal drawings, and other elements of the regular patent application may be included.

The advantages of the PPA are that it costs far less than filing a patent application ($80 as opposed to $370 as of May 2002), doesn't require witnesses, saves the expense of building and testing, and the application is much simpler to complete. If a PPA is filed, the inventor can publish, sell, or show the invention to others without fear of theft or loss of any U.S. rights. That's because anyone who sees and steals the invention would have a later filing date and the inventor would almost certainly be able to win any interference with the thief.

The disadvantages of the PPA are that if the inventor doesn't file a regular patent application within a year of the PPA, the PPA is abandoned and will no longer provide a filing date for purposes of prior-art or interferences. The PPA is worthless if the inventor changes the invention so that it is no longer as described. The filing of a PPA also affects an inventor's foreign rights (see Chapter 9). As with a regular U.S. application, an inventor must pursue foreign patent applications within one year of the PPA's filing date in order to obtain the advantage of the filing date.

In addition to an early filing date and the right to claim patent pending status for an invention, filing a PPA can provide an additional advantage. Since the filing date of the PPA has no effect on the patent's expiration date, the patent's expiration date will still be 20 years from the date the regular patent application is filed. So a PPA has the practical effect of delaying examination of a regular patent application and extending—up to one year—the patent's expiration date. However, the same delaying effect can be obtained if an inventor builds and tests the invention and makes a signed, dated, and witnessed record and delays filing for a year.

F. Trade Secret Considerations

Developing and testing an invention should not compromise the trade secret status of the invention. For example, the notebook should be shown only to those persons willing to maintain its confidentiality. There is an implied understanding that witnesses must maintain confidentiality when signing the lab notebook.

Some inventors prefer that witnesses also sign a confidentiality agreement, sometimes known as a "nondisclosure," "keep-confidential," or "proprietary materials," agreement. These agreements establish a legally binding confidential relationship between the parties. Inventors may also enter into confidentiality agreements with vendors of supplies, prototype makers, manufacturers and companies that want to commercialize the invention. Although a confidentiality agreement will assure the inventor's right to sue someone who discloses confidential information, it will not guarantee success in court. The inventor must also be able to prove that reasonable steps were taken to protect the confidential information and that the information has not become known to the public.

For a nondisclosure (proprietary materials) agreement, see Form 3-1 of *Patent It Yourself*, by David Pressman (Nolo). For more information about nondisclosure agreements, see *Nondislcosure Agreements: Protect Your Trade Secrets and More*, by attorneys Richard Stim and Stephen Fishman (Nolo). ■

Chapter 4

Patent Searching

A. Principles of Patent Searching

Attorneys, inventors, and businesses often need to locate information about patents and related prior-art publications. For example, someone developing an invention may wish to read a specific patent about a similar invention. A company hiring an inventor may want to locate all of the patented inventions created by the new employee. This type of patent search, in which specific items are sought, is referred to as a bibliographic search and can often be done for free with the use of a personal computer hooked to the Internet.

Other types of searches are more complex. For example, a search may be performed to determine if an invention is likely to qualify for a patent. This type of search, referred to as a "patentability search," requires examining current and expired patents and other related prior art to determine if the invention is nonobvious or novel. If the search indicates that an invention is likely to qualify, the inventor can develop, market, license, or sell the invention with some assurance that a patent will issue.

Another type of search, referred to as a "validity search," is made when one company sues another for patent infringement. This type of search is more exhaustive than a patentability search because the company being sued is trying to prove that the PTO made a mistake when it issued the patent and the patent is therefore invalid.

Patentability and validity searches usually require a trip to the PTO in Arlington, Virginia, where paper copies of U.S. patents are arranged by subject matter. For example, all patents that show bicycle hand brakes are physically grouped together, as are all patents that show transistor flip-flop circuits. Also, in the special search areas used by the patent examiners (see Section C2), foreign patents and literature are classified along with U.S. patents according to subject matter.

Although not as thorough, patent searching can be done by using the facilities at the Patent and Trademark Depository Libraries (PTDLs) located in major cities, or by using online patent databases, such as the one at the PTO website, www.uspto.gov. There are limitations to both of these methods and we describe them in Sections C3 and C4.

A search can be performed by a professional searcher (see Section B) or you can do it yourself (see Section C). Some inventors prefer to combine both techniques, for example to do the search themselves and also have a professional search done to double-check their work. Some inventors do a preliminary search, that is locate patents by computer searching, and then hire a professional searcher for a more extensive search.

Patent Searches Are Never Perfect

Even when a professional search is made at the PTO, there are limitations. No search results are 100% certain because:

- there is no way to search pending patent applications with the exception of those published under the 18-month rule (see Chapter 1, Section J)
- if searching through hard copies of patents, some prior-art references can be missing (stolen or borrowed)
- the area being searched may not contain foreign, non-patent, or exotic references
- very recently issued patents may not have been placed in the search files yet
- patents may not be classified in the proper class or classified in an expected way, or
- an invention may have been used publicly (without being published) or it may have been previously invented by an inventor who did not abandon, suppress, or conceal it.

For a comprehensive discussion about patent searching, read *Patent Searching Made Easy*, by David Hitchcock (Nolo).

B. Hiring a Patent Searcher

There are two types of professional patent searchers: those who are licensed to practice before the PTO (patent attorneys and agents) and those who are not licensed. As a general rule, better results are obtained from patent attorneys and patent agents because they understand the concept of nonobviousness and novelty and often dig deeper than might at first appear necessary.

Unlicensed searchers have one big advantage: they charge about half of what most attorneys and agents charge. Before hiring an unlicensed searcher, find out about the searcher's charges, technical background, on-the-job experience, usual amount of time spent on a search, and where the searcher searches (in the PTO's main search room or in the examining division). Most importantly, ask for the names of some clients so that you can check with them. Unlicensed searchers are not authorized to express opinions on patentability.

A "patent agent" has some technical training, generally an undergraduate degree in engineering, and is licensed by the PTO to prepare and prosecute patent applications. A patent agent can conduct a patent search and is authorized to express an opinion on patentability, but cannot appear in court and cannot handle licensing or infringement lawsuits. Patent attorneys must be licensed by the PTO and a licensing authority (such as the state bar or state supreme court) of at least one state. A "general" lawyer licensed to practice in one or more states, but not before the PTO, is not authorized to prepare patent applications or use the title "patent attorney."

Fees for patent searchers range from $100 to $500 for searches by unlicensed searchers; between $300 and $1,200 for searches by licensed patent attorneys or agents, not including an opinion on patentability. Some patent searchers charge a flat fee; others charge by the hour. If you plan to do much of the work yourself, you'll want hourly billing.

1. Locating a Searcher

Most patent searchers can be located in the Yellow Pages of local telephone directories or through Internet search engines (for example, Yahoo.com or Northernlight.com) under "Patent Searchers." Searchers advertise in periodicals such as the *Journal of the Patent and Trademark Office Society*, published by a private association of patent examiners. All patent agents and attorneys are listed in the PTO publication *Attorneys and Agents Registered to Practice Before the U.S. Patent and Trademark Office* (A&ARTP), available in many public libraries, Patent and Trademark Depository Libraries (see Section C3 below), government bookstores,

and on the PTO's website, www.uspto.gov. Most patent attorneys and agents who do searching in the PTO can be found in the District of Columbia section, or the Virginia section of A&ARTP under zip code 22202. Generally, hiring an attorney or agent in your locality to do the search is very inefficient and costly since the attorney or agent will have to hire an associate in or travel to Arlington to make the search.

2. Preparing the Searcher

When furnishing a search request to a searcher, include the following:

- a clear and complete description of the invention
- drawings
- a copy of a related patent to identify the appropriate class to be searched
- identification of the novel features, and
- any required deadlines.

If using a patent attorney or agent, a search request will not compromise any trade-secret status of the invention since by law it's considered a confidential communication. This simply means that the patent attorney or agent is required to keep your invention a secret. If using an unlicensed searcher, the law does not presume the disclosure is confidential, so you should ask your searcher to sign a confidentiality agreement, a contract in which one or both parties agree not to disclose certain information.

A copy of the inventor's notebook or invention disclosure can be sent to the searcher. To guard against theft, we recommend blanking out all dates on any document provided to the searcher.

3. Reviewing the Search Results

After completing a search, a searcher usually furnishes:

- a list of the patents and other references discovered during the search
- a brief discussion of the cited patents and other references, pointing out the relevant parts of each, and
- a list of the classes and subclasses searched and the examiners consulted, if any.

The searcher will enclose copies of the references (usually U.S. patents, but possibly also foreign patents, magazine articles, and other published materials) cited in the search report. (For information about reading a patent, see Chapter 5.) If a patent attorney or agent has been hired to search, they will render an opinion as to patentability for an additional fee, usually $200 to $400.

The determination of whether an invention is patentable is rarely a "yes" or "no" answer, unless the invention is a very simple device, process, or composition. Many inventions are complex enough to have some features, or some combination of features, that will be different enough to be patentable. However, the inventor's goal is not merely to get a patent, but to get meaningful patent coverage—that is, offensive rights that are broad enough that competitors can't "design around" the patent easily. Designing around a patent is the act of making a competitive device or process that is equivalent in function to the patented device but that doesn't infringe the patent.

After the search results are evaluated, the inventor has a pretty good idea of the minimum number of novel features that are necessary to sufficiently distinguish the invention over the prior art. The scope of patent coverage—that is, how narrow or broad the claims—is determined by the novel features that distinguish an invention over the prior art and provide new results that are different or unexpected enough to be considered nonobvious. The fewer the novel features needed to distinguish the invention, the broader the scope of coverage. Stated differently, if many new features are needed to distinguish the invention from prior art, the coverage is narrow and it's usually easier for a competitor to provide the same results without infringing.

C. Do It Yourself Searching

The most thorough searches are done at the PTO in Arlington, Virginia. The PTO libraries are open to the public and any inventor can travel to Arlington and perform a search using the PTO files. Although not as thorough, searches can also be performed using the facilities of PTDLs located in major U.S. cities, or by using online patent databases. The limitations of these methods are discussed below.

1. Search Prerequisites: Terminology and Classification

Regardless of whether you are performing a simple search or an extensive search, there are two prerequisites: you must articulate the terms that describe the nature and essence of the invention, and then find the relevant classifications or Boolean search terms for the invention.

In order to properly search for patents, you must be familiar with the elements of a patent, such as the specification, claims, and abstract. For information on patent elements, read Chapter 5.

a. Terms That Describe the Invention

In the PTO files, patents, like any indexed system, are classified using keywords (terms) and classifications. Successful patent searching is dependent on using the same words and phrases that coincide with the terms used by the PTO classifier or indexer. For example, if artificial rainmaking machines are indexed by "rainfall simulation," you will have a difficult time locating patents under "artificial rain." For this reason, you must first figure out several ways to describe the invention and extract the terminology from those descriptions in order to locate similar inventions. For

example, if you're searching for patents relating to a bicycle with a new type of sprocket wheel, write down "bicycle, sprocket wheel," and any additional terms. In the computer search systems at the PTO and elsewhere, these terms are called Boolean terms because the computer searches for relevant patents using Boolean logic. Boolean logic is a searching method in which terms are joined by using connectors such as AND, OR, and NOT (for example, "Bicycle AND Wheel"). Boolean searching is explained in greater detail in Section C4b, below.

b. Classification for the Invention

In addition to appropriate terminology, you also need to determine the invention's most relevant search classification, called class and subclass. Every type of invention is categorized in a class. For example, if you invented something that has to do with sewing, you would search in Class 112. If the invention had to do with sewing gloves, it would be in Class 112, Subclass 16. You can find the appropriate classifications in any of the following references, all of which are available in hard copy, on CD-ROM, or at the PTO website. These consist of:

- ***Index to the U.S. Patent Classification.*** Lists all possible subject areas of invention alphabetically, from "abacus" to "zwieback," together with the appropriate class and subclass for each. The *Index* also lists the classes alphabetically.

- *Manual of Classification.* Lists all classes numerically and subclasses under each class. After locating the class and subclass numbers, the *Manual of Classification* is used as an adjunct to the *Index* to check the selected classes and to find other, closely related ones.
- *Classification Definitions.* Contains a definition for every class and subclass in the *Manual of Classification*. At the end of each subclass definition is a cross-reference to additional places to look that correspond to the subclass. A local PTDL will have the Classification And Search Support Information System (CASSIS) on CD-ROM, where search classifications can be found.

2. Searching at the PTO

The PTO is physically located at South 23rd Street and U.S. 1 (Jefferson Davis Highway) in Arlington, Virginia, about half-a-mile west of the Washington National Airport. Although the PTO is technically part of the Department of Commerce (headquartered in Washington, D.C.), it operates in an almost autonomous fashion. The first floor of the main PTO building (Crystal Plaza 4) contains the main search room. The various examining divisions and administration departments are upstairs in this and adjacent buildings. The primary advantage of searching at the PTO is that you have access to printed and microfiche copies of all U.S.

patents arranged according to their classifications, as well as patent assignments and examiner's search files.

Access to patent paper files, CD-ROM products, and assignment search systems is available to the public without charge. Staff members can assist customers in locating appropriate files and reference materials. In addition to patent copies, the PTO search facilities maintain a variety of reference materials, including manuals, indices, dictionaries, reference publications, and the *Official Gazette*. The *Official Gazette* is published each Tuesday to announce those patents being issued and those trademarks being registered or published for opposition. Volumes relating specifically to patents or trademarks are available in the corresponding search facility.

The PTO employs about 1,200 examiners, all of whom have technical undergraduate degrees in such fields as electrical engineering, chemistry, or physics. Many examiners are also attorneys. Examiners review patent applications and determine whether inventions meet the standard of patentability. The PTO also has about an equal number of clerical, supervisory, and support personnel. Assuming you do go to the PTO in Arlington, here's what you'll find. There are two places you can make the search:

- the public search room, referred to as the Public Patent Search and Image Retrieval Facility (PSIRF), and
- the examiners' search files in the actual examining division.

Most searchers make their search in the public search room on the first floor where there are search tables. However, we recommend going upstairs to the examiners' search files because examiners are there to assist you, literature and foreign patents are available, it's much quieter, and the patent files are likely to be more intact. To get into the upstairs search room, you must apply for a user pass, which will take only a few minutes. You must also ask permission from an examiner or clerk before starting the particular search.

If you need help with the search, you can ask any of the search assistants in the search room or, even better, an examiner in the actual examining division. The security of the invention won't be endangered by providing the details. Employees of the PTO are not allowed to file patent applications.

3. Searching in a Patent and Trademark Depository Library

If you can't make it to Virginia, the next best possibility is to search in one of the Patent and Trademark Depository Libraries listed on the PTO website (www.uspto.gov). Before going to any PTDL, call to find out their hours of operation and what search facilities they have.

Searches using PTDL resources are less thorough than the PTO because not all PTDLs have all U.S. patents and none of them have patents arranged by subject matter into searchable classifications (as does the PTO in Arlington). PTDLs generally do not have foreign patents or non-patent literature (books, magazines, and other published materials). Using a PTDL is generally more difficult and time-consuming than using the PTO facilities in Virginia.

The PTO periodically publishes CD-ROM disks that contain information about patents. All PTDLs subscribe to these disks and have one or more computers with CD-ROM drives for reading the disks. Because the disks only contain classification and bibliographic information, they can't be used to make a true patentability search. They can be used as a searching aid and to provide other information about patents that you may find useful. The two most helpful disks are:

- **CASSIS/CLASS** disks (cover patents from 1790 to the present) can be used to find the classification of any patent, or the list of patents in any class.

- **CASSIS/BIB** disks (cover patents from 1980 to the present) can be used to find the classification of any recently issued patent, to find all patents assigned to any company or individual, to find a list of patents by year of issue, status (expired, reexamined, etc.), all patents by inventor's residence, all recently issued patents with a certain word or words in their title or abstract (this feature can be used to perform a crude search), and to find the field of search (class and subclass) for any type of invention.

Searching the *Official Gazette*

The *Official Gazette* for patents (the OG) is a thick periodical published weekly by the PTO, listing the main facts (patentee, assignee, filing date, classification) plus the broadest claim and main drawing figure of every patent issued that week. It also contains pertinent notices, fees, and a list of all PTDLs. It is possible to perform a preliminary search using the OG located at a PTDL (or at the PTO) and it is generally easier than using CASSIS because each patent entry in the OG only contains a single claim (or abstract) and a single figure or drawing of the patent, as indicated in Fig. 4A below (a typical page from an OG).

PTDLs maintain copies of the OG in print or on microfiche. For each patent, the OG entry gives the patent number, inventor's name and address, assignee (usually a company that the inventor has transferred ownership of the patent to), filing date, application serial number, international classification, U.S. classification, number of claims, and a sample claim or abstract. If the drawing and claim look relevant, go to the actual patent online or order a copy of it. The claim found in the *Official Gazette* is the essence of the claimed invention, not a descriptive summary of the technical information in the patent. Therefore, even if a patent's *Official Gazette* claim doesn't precisely describe the invention, the rest of the patent may still be relevant. If you can't get to a PTDL, most large public or university libraries subscribe to the *Official Gazette*.

Obtaining Copies of Patents

You can order a copy of a patent by:

- writing a letter listing the number of the patent to Commissioner of Patents and Trademarks, Washington, DC 20231, with a check for the price per patent (see Fee Schedule at the PTO website) times the total number of patents you've ordered; or by clicking "Order Copy" at the "Manual Search" page at the PTO website, www.uspto.gov
- filling out a PTO patent copy order coupon if using the facilities at a PTDL
- downloading a text copy or image copy of the patent from the PTO search site, or
- ordering a copy from a private supply company, such as Faxpat, www.faxpat.com, or Delphion, www.delphion.com.

4. Computer Searching

Computer searching is ideal for locating a specific patent and performing preliminary research but, by itself, is not suitable for determining patentability or validity. This is because the patents in most computer search data banks usually go back only to 1971 or 1976, and it is possible that a patent issued before these dates might demonstrate the obviousness or lack of novelty for a

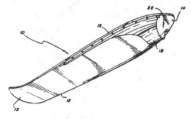

c) at least one groove provided in said flange, said groove facing said opening in said nipple for providing water communication between said groove and said opening in said nipple at an amply low and fairly constant total head; and

d) wherein at some point said groove is narrower than the diameter of said bore.

6,089,934

ENGINE COOLING SYSTEM WITH SIMPLIFIED DRAIN AND FLUSHING PROCEDURE

Timothy M. Biggs, Stillwater; William E. Hughes, Perry; Matthew W. Jaeger, Stillwater; Andrew K. Logan, Stillwater; Robert J. Pitchford, Stillwater, and Charles E. Wright, Stillwater, all of Okla., assignors to Brunswick Corporation, Lake Forest, Ill.

Filed Jul. 26, 1999, Appl. No. 361,370
Int. Cl.[7] B63H 21/10

U.S. Cl. 440—88   20 Claims

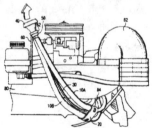

1. An engine cooling system, comprising:

a first opening extending through a first portion of said engine and into said cooling system;

a first flexible conduit having a first end connected in fluid communication with said first opening;

a retainer movably attached to said first flexible conduit and movable between said first end of said first flexible conduit and a second end of said first flexible conduit;

a handle;

a tether attached between said handle and said retainer; and

whereby said second end of said first flexible conduit is movable, in response to manual movement of said handle, from a first position above said first opening to a second position below said first opening.

6,089,935

WATER SKI ATTACHMENT

G. Thomas Fleming, III, 5111 Alta Canyada Rd., La Canada, Calif. 91011

Filed Feb. 6, 1998, Appl. No. 135,511
Int. Cl.[7] B63B 35/81

U.S. Cl. 441—79   10 Claims

1. A water ski comprising:

an upper side, an under side, a front end and a rear end, with an arched fin carried on said ski under side at said ski rear end;

said arched fin having opposed edges adjacent the edges of said ski under side, with said opposed edges joined together adjacent said ski rear end to form an opening for water flow therethrough; and

with said opposed edges tapering forward and upward from said opening to said ski under side, and terminating forward of said ski rear end, the opposing edges of said ski converge toward each other at the rear portion of said ski, and the opposing edges of said arched fin conform to said edges of said ski.

6,089,936

PERSONAL FLOATATION DEVICE

Richard S. Hoffman, 6749 SW. 166 Dr., Pembroke Pines, Fla. 33331

Filed Mar. 5, 1999, Appl. No. 263,350
Int. Cl.[7] B63C 9/08

U.S. Cl. 441—117   26 Claims

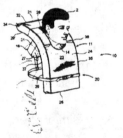

1. A float for a personal flotation device, said float comprising:

a) a front formed of a buoyant material, said front sized to generally correspond and confront a wearer's chest and shoulder region;

b) said front including a neck opening sized and configured to permit passage of the wearer's head therethrough and defining a recess surface about said neck opening;

c) a back formed of buoyant material, said back having a first end, a second end and a body between said ends;

d) said back being movably connected to said front with said first end of said back disposed generally adjacent said recess surface and so as to reduce an inner diameter of said neck opening;

e) said back being movable between a position wherein said neck opening is opened sufficiently to permit the wearer's head to pass therethrough and another position wherein said back confronts the wearer's back region;

f) said body of said back being sized and configured to generally confront the wearer's upper and central back region and to dwell within said neck opening; and

g) said back being movable into another position closing said neck opening.

Figure 4A—Page from *Official Gazette* Showing Various Patent Abstracts

new invention. This is not a problem for most high-tech inventions because the relevant prior art is post-1960s.

Despite its weaknesses, computer searching has some obvious advantages, such as cost and ease of use. We will explain some computer searching techniques and differentiate the various patent databases.

a. Computer Search Resources

In order to perform computer searching, you must have access to certain databases. This is done either with a personal computer with Internet access or via an existing terminal that is dedicated to patent searching, such as at a PTDL, large company, law firm, or in the PTO. In this section we focus on the databases that are available using personal computers with Internet access.

Free database:
- **The U.S. Patent & Trademark Office,** www.uspto.gov. The PTO website has a full-text searchable database of patents and drawings that cover the period from January 1976 to the most recent weekly issue date (usually each Tuesday).

Fee-based databases:
- **Delphion,** www.delphion.com. The Delphion website has evolved from the former IBM patent website. The site offers U.S. patents searchable from 1971 to the present and (and it is expected to add pre-1971 patents) as well as full text patents from the European Patent Office, the World Intellectual Property Organization PCT collection and abstracts from Derwent World Patent Index (which includes 40 international patent-issuing authorities).
- **Micropatent,** www.micropatent.com. The Micropatent website offers U.S. and Japanese patents searchable from 1976 to the present, International PCT patents from 1983, European patents from 1988, and the *Official Gazette* for patents.
- **LexPat,** www.lexis-nexis.com. LexPat provides U.S. patents searchable from 1971 to the present. In addition, the LEXPAT library offers extensive prior-art searching capability of technical journals and magazines.
- **QPAT,** www.qpat.com. The QPAT website offers U.S. patents searchable from 1974 to the present.

Several of the "for fee" databases provide foreign patent information. For more information on searching foreign patents, review the links at http://patent.search-in.net/. (For more information about foreign patents and their importance, see Chapter 9.)

 Viewing drawings at the PTO site. The PTO website provides patent drawings, but your Internet browser must be capable of viewing a specific type of TIFF image known as a G4 compression TIFF.

Many browsers cannot read this TIFF format. If you are having problems viewing patent drawings from the PTO website, link to www.uspto.gov/web/menu/viewers.html, where the PTO provides information about where to obtain a downloadable TIFF viewer.

b.   Computer Searching Terminology

Most computer search systems do not group and search patents by PTO classification. Instead, they search solely for combinations of key words in the text of the patent, a method of searching known as "Boolean searching."

For example, consider a bicycle invention with a frame made of a certain carbon-fiber alloy. If searching at the PTO, the searcher would look through the patents in the bike and metallurgical (carbon-fiber alloy) classifications. However, if searching for the same invention online, the searcher would select a combination of key words (such as "bicycle" and "carbon fiber alloy") and the search engine would identify any patents that contain the key words.

The search may result in finding too many irrelevant patents, in which case the search can be narrowed by using more specific key words. However, if the search words are too specific, the search engine is likely to report no patents, or just one or two. The PTO's examiners presently use computer searching to supplement their searches.

Before searching a database, thoroughly study the service's instruction manual or online help program. If using a fee-based database, this will help to keep costs down. Although every system is different, the following terms are common to all systems.

- **File.** The actual name of the patent search database provided by the service (for example, LEXPAT is the name and trademark for Mead Data's patent database and CLAIMS is Dialog's patent database).
- **Record.** A portion of a file. The term is used to designate a single reference, usually a patent, within the database.
- **Field.** A portion of a record, such as a patent's title, the names of the inventors, its filing date, its patent number, its claims, and more.
- **Term.** A group or, in computer-speak, a "string" of characters within a field (for example, the inventor's surname or one word of the patent title are all terms).
- **Command.** An instruction or directive to the search system that tells it to perform a function (for example, "Search" might be a command to tell a system to look for some key words in its database).
- **Key Word or Search Term.** Words that are actually searched (for example, "bicycle" and "carbon fiber alloy" are key words we've used in examples above).

- **Qualifier.** A symbol that is used to limit a search or the information that the search displays. Normally no qualifier would be used in novelty searches, but if you're looking for a patent from a certain inventor, you could add a qualifier that limits your search to the field of the inventor's name.
- **Wild Card Symbol.** A symbol that is used in place of a word's normal ending in order to broaden a key word (for example, if the wild card were an asterisk (*) and you typed "Auto*" your search would display "automobile," "automotive," "automatic," and any other word that started with the prefix "auto").
- **Connector Word.** A word such as "OR," "AND," and "NOT" that tells the computer to look for certain defined logical or Boolean combinations of key words. For instance, if you type in a command telling the computer to search for "annulus OR ring AND napkin," the computer would recognize that "OR" and "AND" were connector words, and would search for patents with the words "annulus" and "napkin," or "ring" and "napkin," in combination.
- **Proximity Symbol.** Tells the computer to look for specified key words, provided they are not more than a certain number of terms apart. Thus, if you told the computer to search for "napkin w/5 shaping" it would look for any patent that contained the words "napkin" and "shaping" within five words of each other, the symbol "w/5" meaning "within five words of." If no proximity symbol is used and the words are placed adjacent to each other—such as "napkin shaping"—the computer will retrieve only those patents that contain these two words adjacent to each other in the order given. However, if a connector word is used—such as "napkin AND shaping"—the computer will pull out any patent with both of these words, no matter where they are in the patent and no matter in what order they appear.

c. Alternative Search Terms

No matter what online search system you use, be prepared with a group of key words and possible synonyms or equivalents. Use a thesaurus or a visual dictionary to get synonyms. Thus, to search for a napkin-shaping ring, in addition to the obvious key words "ring," "napkin," and "shaping," think of other terms from the same and analogous fields. In addition to napkin, you could use "cloth." Or, in addition to shaping, you could use "folding" or "bending."

Prior Art for Software Patents

The question of novelty and nonobviousness for software inventions is vexing. Many practitioners argue that the PTO has wrongly issued many software and Internet patents. In order to fortify a validity or patentability search for a software invention, it is wise to go beyond a search of patent files and diligently search other prior-art sources. One repository of software prior art is the Software Patent Institute, www.spi.org. Although the SPI does not maintain a patent database, it does contain a comprehensive database of related prior-art references for software, such as computer manuals, older textbooks and journal articles, conference proceedings, computer science theses, and other such materials that can function as "pointers" to prior art.

d. Patent Searching Techniques

To give you an idea of how online searching works, let's proceed through a search using the PTO's patent database. To begin any search at the PTO website, access the home page at www.uspto.gov, and then click "Patents" or "Search Patents." You are directed to a screen entitled "Patent Full-Text and Full-Page Image Databases." You can elect to search either "Patent Grants" for current patents or "Patent Applications" if you wish to search published patent applications. Let's assume you were searching for prior-art patents related to hot-air popcorn poppers. There are three ways to search both databases, Boolean Search, Manual Search, and Patent Number Search.

- **Boolean Search.** This type of search is accomplished by using terms, fields. and connectors. In section C4b, we described some of the principles of Boolean searching such as the use of wild cards, connectors, and proximity symbols. You must also select a year or range of years to search from the database. If you do not select a range of years, the search will default to the last year of issued patents.

As you can see from Fig 4C, the Boolean searching system has been simplified to some extent so you can select the connector term ("AND," "OR," "AND NOT") from a drop-down menu. You can initiate a search for hot-air popcorn poppers by searching for patents with the words "popcorn AND air" anywhere in the patent.

- **Manual Search.** The Manual Search Page allows you to query the patent database using "command line search syntax," a fancy title for searching the different portions of the patent. For example, if you want to find all patents with the word "popcorn" and the word "air" in the claims, you would locate the field codes for the claims (ACLM) and create a search, such as "ACLM/air" and "ACLM/popcorn." The primary advantage of the Manual Search over Boolean searching is that you can search more than two fields

UNITED STATES PATENT AND TRADEMARK OFFICE

| Home | Index | Search | System Alerts | eBusiness Center | News & Notices | Contact Us |

USPTO

Patent Full-Text and Full-Page Image Databases

Patent Grants
(full-text since 1976, full-page images since 1790)

- Quick Search
- Advanced Search
- Patent Number Search

- Help
- How to Access Full-Page Images

Patent Applications
(published since 15 March 2001)

- Quick Search
- Advanced Search
- Application Number Search

- Help
- How to Access Full-Page Images

- Tools to Help in Searching by Patent Classification

Important Notices Concerning These Databases:

- These databases are intended for use by the general public. Due to limitations of equipment and bandwidth, they are not intended to be a source for bulk downloads of USPTO data. Bulk data may be purchased from USPTO at cost (see the USPTO Products and Services Catalog). Individuals, companies, IP addresses, or blocks of IP addresses who, in effect, deny service to the general public by generating unusually high numbers (1000 or more) of daily database accesses (searches, pages, or hits), whether generated manually or in an automated fashion, may be denied access to these servers without notice.

- If you can access this page, but cannot successfully access any of the Quick Search, Advanced Boolean Searching, or Patent Number Searching pages linked above, your workstation or organization may have been denied access to the Web Patent Databases. To determine if you have been denied access, or to seek to have your access restored, send email including your workstation and firewall or gateway IP addresses to larson@uspto.gov. Consult with your network administrators if necessary, as email without the required IP addresses cannot be processed.

Figure 4B—PTO Web Patent Database

US PATENT & TRADEMARK OFFICE
PATENT FULL TEXT AND IMAGE DATABASE

| Help | Home | Boolean | Manual | Number | Order Copy | PTDLs |

Shopping Cart

Data current through 03/28/2000

Query [Help]

Term 1: [_____]   in **Field 1:** [All Fields ▾]

[AND ▾]

Term 2: [_____]   in **Field 2:** [All Fields ▾]

Select years [Help] [1999-2000 ▾]   [Search]   [Reset]

Figure 4C—Boolean Search

or use more than two search terms at one time. As with the Boolean searches, you must also select a year or range of years to search from the database. The field codes are identified in each search page at the PTO website.

- **Patent Number Search.** The simplest way to locate a patent is if you have its number. Simply click "Patent Number Search" and type in the number. The search results are then provided and you can view the text file of the patent by clicking on its name. For example, if you wanted to view the design patent for a hot-air popcorn popper and only had the number, you would type in the number in the search field and the text of the patent would be displayed. You can view the actual images by clicking "Images," provided you have a TIFF reader on your computer. ■

Chapter 5

Reading and Writing Patents

Patents are written in a formal, stylized manner and have parts that use arcane language packed with legal and scientific terminology. That's the bad news. The good news is that any patent can be interpreted with patience. The purpose of this chapter is to introduce you to the various elements of a patent and discuss how a patent application is prepared.

A. Elements of a Patent

The key elements of a patent are: (1) data about the inventor, serial number, dates and related information, (2) the specification, (3) the claims, (4) the abstract, and (5) the drawings. The drawings and the specification explain how to make and use the invention and the claims define the scope or boundaries of the patent. Specifications for patents issued since 1971 must include an abstract that summarizes the invention. All patent applications must include a drawing if the subject matter permits. However, some applications, such as for pure chemicals, don't include a drawing unless a process can be diagrammed by a flowchart. We will discuss these five elements in the following sections. In Section G, we will discuss additional materials required when submitting a patent application.

B. Invention and Inventor Data

The first page of the patent provides the inventor's name, the name of the assignee (the person or company to whom the inventor transferred ownership), the application date, the application serial number, the patent date, the patent number, any related prior applications, the field of invention that was searched and any relevant prior art cited in the search (see Chapter 4).

C. Specification

The specification basically discloses how to make and use an invention. Every specification must describe the invention so that someone knowledgeable in the field of the invention can make and use it without any further experimenting. The specification must also disclose the "best mode," or the best way, of creating and using the invention. If the inventor knew of a better way and failed to disclose it, that failure could result in the loss of patent rights.

> EXAMPLE: In 1978, an inventor at United States Gypsum (USG) conceived of a formula for a joint compound. A joint compound is used to fill the joints between adjacent gypsum wallboards. One of the ingredients in the formula was a silicon-treated substance called Sil-42. When discussing the compound with USG's patent attorney, the inventor listed Sil-42 as a component, but before

the patent application was filed, a USG executive instructed the attorney to omit any reference to Sil-42. After the patent issued, USG sued National Gypsum for infringement of its joint compound patent. The court held that the patent was invalid because, by omitting the silicon substance, USG failed to disclose the best mode of making the joint compound. (*United States Gypsum Co. v. National Gypsum Co.*, 74 F.3d 1209 (CAFC 1996).)

1. Elements of the Specification

According to PTO Rule 77 (37 CFR 1.77), the specification should consist of the following elements:

- title
- cross-reference to related application(s) (if any)
- federally sponsored research and development (if any)
- sequence listing or program (if any; usually includes a biotechnological sequence or a computer program)
- background of the invention (usually includes a discussion of prior art and the objects and advantages of the invention)
- summary (usually a one-paragraph description of the invention)
- description of drawings
- detailed description of the invention and how it works
- computer program (if any)

- claims and abstract (although legally part of the specification, popular usage and this book treat them as separate parts of the application; see Sections D and E), and
- sequence listing for biotech inventions (if any).

The specification is supposed to have separate headings in capital letters (but not in boldface). The specification elements shown here reflect changes made in patent rules in 2000. Applications filed prior to this change include the same information although the headings in the published patent may differ.

Throughout this section, we will isolate each element of the specification and provide an example from a patent titled "Paper-Laminated Pliable Closure for Flexible Bags" (Pat. No. 4,783,886).

2. Title

The title is a short, simple summary of the invention, for example "Paper-Laminated Pliable Closure for Flexible Bags" (Pat. No. 4,783,886). (See Fig. 5A, below.)

Patent Numbers. Every U.S. patent since 1836 has been issued a patent number, for example, Pat. No. 5,152,062. Patent numbering started in 1836 and patent 6,000,000 issued in December 1999. When several patents are the subjects of litigation or interference, judges and attorneys refer to each patent by the last three digits of the registration, for example, the 062 patent.

indicated here and included, either in the specification or on a CD.

3. Cross-References to Related Applications

If the inventor or an inventor in the same organization has any other patent applications on file relating to the current invention, these are listed in the Cross-References section. Cross-references are necessary if the applicant is seeking the benefit of the filing date of a prior application or wants to incorporate a disclaimer of another case. (See Chapter 6, Section B3, for more information about when a cross-reference may be useful.) If there are no cross-references, this section can be omitted or the applicant may state, "Not applicable."

4. Federally Sponsored Research and Development

If the invention was made with government funding, the government will have rights in the invention and this will be indicated here. A typical statement may read, "This invention was made under a contract with the U.S. Department of Energy."

5. Sequence Listing or Program

If the invention uses a biotechnological sequence or a computer program, it will be

6. Background (Field of the Invention)

In this section, the applicant categorizes the invention by type of product or technology.

This invention relates to plastic tab closures. Specifically, it relates to such closures used for closing the necks of plastic produce bags.

7. Background (Discussion of Prior Art)

In order to demonstrate novelty and non-obviousness, the invention must be distinguished from prior art. This usually means that prior inventions are criticized.

Grocery stores and supermarkets commonly supply consumers with polyethylene bags for holding produce. Such bags are also used by suppliers to provide a resealable container for other items, both edible and inedible.
Originally these bags were sealed by the supplier with staples or by heat. However, consumers objected since these were of a rather permanent nature: the bags could be opened only by tearing, thereby damaging them and rendering them impossible to reseal.

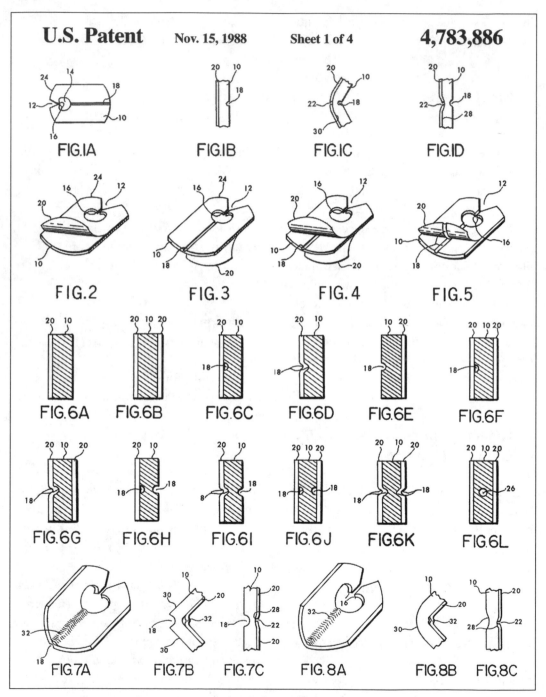

Figure 5A—Drawings of Sample Patent Application

Thereafter, inventors created several types of closures to seal plastic bags in such a way as to leave them undamaged after they were opened. U.S. patent 4,292,714 to Walker (1981) discloses a complex clamp which can close the necks of bags without causing damage upon opening; however, these clamps are prohibitively expensive to manufacture.

U.S. patent number 2,981,990 to Balderree (1961) shows a closure which is of expensive construction, being made of PTFE, and which is not effective unless the bag has a relatively long "neck." Thus if the bag has been filled almost completely and consequently has a short neck, this closure is useless. Also, being relatively narrow and clumsy, Balderree's closure cannot be easily bent by hand along its longitudinal axis. Finally, his closure does not hold well onto the bag, but has a tendency to snap off.

Although twist closures with a wire core are easy to use and inexpensive to manufacture, do not damage the bag upon being removed, and can be used repeatedly, they simply do not possess the neat and uniform appearance of a tab closure. They become tattered and unsightly after repeated use and do not offer suitable surfaces for the reception of print or labeling. These ties also require much more manipulation to apply and remove.

Several types of thin, flat closures have been proposed—for example, in U.K. patent 883,771 to Britt et al. (1961) and U.S. patents 3,164,250 (1965), 3,417,912

(1968), 3,822,441 (1974), 4,361,935 (1982), and 4,509,231 (1985), all to Paxton. Although inexpensive to manufacture, capable of use with bags having a short neck, and producible in break-off strips, such closures can be used only once if they are made of frangible plastic since they must be bent or twisted when being removed and consequently will fracture upon removal. Thus, to reseal a bag originally sealed with a frangible closure, one must either close its neck with another closure or else close it in makeshift fashion by folding or tying it. My own patent 4,694,542 (1987) describes a closure which is made of flexible plastic and is therefore capable of repeated use without damage to the bag, but nevertheless all the plastic closures heretofore known suffer from a number of disadvantages:

(a) Their manufacture in color requires the use of a compounding facility for the production of the pigmented plastic. Such a facility, which is needed to compound the primary pigments and which generally constitutes a separate production site, requires the presence of very large storage bins for the pigmented raw granules. Also, it presents great difficulties with regard to the elimination of the airborne powder which results from the mixing of the primary granules.

(b) If one uses an extruder in the production of a pigmented plastic— especially if one uses only a single

extruder—a change from one color to a second requires purging the extruder of the granules having the first color by introducing those of the second color. This process inevitably produces, in sizeable volume, an intermediate product of an undesired color which must be discarded as scrap, thereby resulting in waste of material and time.

(c) The colors of the closures in present use are rather unsaturated. If greater concentrations of pigment were used in order to make the colors more intense, the plastic would become more brittle and the cost of the final product would increase.

(d) The use of pigmented plastic closures does not lend itself to the production of multicolored designs, and it would be very expensive to produce plastic closures in which the plastic is multicolored—for example, in which the plastic has stripes of several colors, or in which the plastic exhibits multicolored designs.

(e) Closures made solely of plastic generally offer poor surfaces for labeling or printing, and the label or print is often easily smudged.

(f) The printing on a plastic surface is often easily erased, thereby allowing the alteration of prices by dishonest consumers.

(g) The plastic closures in present use are slippery when handled with wet or greasy fingers.

(b) A closure of the type in present use can be very carefully pried off a bag by a dishonest consumer and then attached to another item without giving any evidence of such removal.

8. Objects and Advantages

In the patent field, the term "objects" means "what the invention accomplishes." Usually, the objects are also the invention's advantages since those aspects are intended to be superior over prior art. In some ways, this section is the converse of the disadvantages described in the prior art discussion (see Section C7, above).

Accordingly, besides the objects and advantages of the flexible closures described in my above patent, several objects and advantages of the present invention are:

(a) to provide a closure which can be produced in a variety of colors without requiring the manufacturer to use a compounding facility for the production of pigments

(b) to provide a closure whose production allows for a convenient and extremely rapid and economical change of color in the closures that are being produced

(c) to provide a closure which both is flexible and can be brightly colored

(d) to provide a closure which can be colored in several colors simultaneously

(e) to provide a closure which will present a superior surface for the reception of labeling or print

(f) to provide a closure whose labeling cannot be altered

(g) to provide a closure which will not be slippery when handled with wet or greasy fingers; and

(h) to provide a closure which will show evidence of having been switched from one item to another by a dishonest consumer—in other words, to provide a closure which makes items tamper-proof.

Further objects and advantages are to provide a closure which can be used easily and conveniently to open and reseal a plastic bag, without damage to the bag, which is simple to use and inexpensive to manufacture, which can be supplied in separate tabs en masse or in break-off links, which can be used with bags having short necks, which can be used repeatedly, and which obviates the need to tie a knot in the neck of the bag or fold the neck under the bag or use a twist closure. Still further objects and advantages will become apparent from a consideration of the ensuing description and drawings.

9. Summary

The specification must contain a summary of the invention.

The bag closure comprises a flat body having a notch, a gripping aperture adjacent the notch and a layer of paper laminated on its side.

10. Drawings

The description of the drawings provides detailed explanations for the different portions (or "figures") of the patent drawing. For more information on drawings, see Section F.

In the drawings, closely related figures have the same number but different alphabetic suffixes.

Figs 1A to 1D show various aspects of a closure supplied with a longitudinal groove and laminated on one side with paper.

Fig 2 shows a closure with no longitudinal groove and with a paper lamination on one side only.

Fig 3 shows a similar closure with one longitudinal groove.

Fig 4 shows a similar closure with a paper lamination on both sides.

Fig 5 shows a similar closure with a paper lamination on one side only, the groove having been formed into the paper as well as into the body of the closure.

Figs 6A to 6K show end views of closures having various combinations of paper laminations, longitudinal grooves, and through-holes.

Figs 7A to 7C show a laminated closure with groove after being bent and after being straightened again.

Figs 8A to 8C show a laminated closure without a groove after being bent and after being straightened again.

11. Detailed Description

This section describes the invention's structure and explains its performance. Usually, the description and operation are provided in two separate subparts, as reproduced below, but some inventions are not capable of physical descriptions and the two sections (description and operation) are merged, for example, as in a chemical process.

Description of Invention—Preferred Embodiment. The description is a discussion of the invention's physical structure or static arrangement. It usually starts with the base, frame, bottom, input, or some other logical starting place of the invention, and then works up, out, or forward in a logical manner. Each part is named and numbered and is usually related to the numbering in the patent drawings. Previously, we explained that the specification must provide the best mode or embodiment of the invention. It is in this portion of the specification that the best mode is provided.

A preferred embodiment of the closure of the present invention is illustrated in Fig 1A (top view) and Fig 1B (end view). The closure has a thin base 10 of uniform cross section consisting of a flexible sheet of material which can be repeatedly bent and straightened out without fracturing. A layer of paper 20 (Fig 1B) is laminated on one side of base 10. In the preferred embodiment, the base is a flexible plastic, such as poly-ethylene-tere-phthalate (PET—hyphens here supplied to facilitate pronunciation)—available from Eastman Chemical Co. of Kingsport, TN. However, the base can consist of any other material that can be repeatedly bent without fracturing, such as polyethylene, polypropylene, vinyl, nylon, rubber, leather, various impregnated or laminated fibrous materials, various plasticized materials, cardboard, paper, etc.

At one end of the closure is a lead-in notch 12 which terminates in gripping points 16 and leads to a hole 14. Paper layer 20 adheres to base 10 by virtue either of the extrusion of liquid plastic (which will form the body of the closure) directly onto the paper or the application of heat or adhesive upon the entirety of one side of base 10. The paper-laminated closure is then punched out. Thus the lamination will have the same shape as the side of the base 10 to which it adheres.

The base of the closure is typically .8 mm to 1.2 mm in thickness, and has overall dimensions roughly from 20 mm x 20 mm (square shape) to 40 mm x 70 mm (oblong shape). The outer four corners 24 of the closure are typically beveled or rounded to avoid snagging and personal injury. Also, when closure tabs are connected side-to-side in a long roll, these bevels or roundings give the roll a series of notches which act as detents or indices for the positioning and conveying of the tabs in a dispensing machine.

A longitudinal groove 18 is formed on one side of base 10 in Fig 1. In other embodiments, there may be two longitudinal grooves—one on each side of the base—or there may be no longitudinal groove at all. Groove 18 may be formed by machining, scoring, rolling, or extruding. In the absence of a groove, there may be a longitudinal through-hole 26 (Fig 6L). This through-hole may be formed by placing, in the extrusion path of the closure, a hollow pin for the outlet of air.

Description of Additional or Alternative Embodiments. If an invention can be embodied or operated in several ways, the specification should describe the most preferred or most basic embodiment and its operation first, then describe each additional or alternative embodiment in the same manner, but more briefly.

Additional embodiment

Additional embodiments are shown in Figs 2, 3, 4, and 5; in each case the paper lamination is shown partially peeled back. In Fig 2 the closure has only one lamination and no groove; in Fig 3 it has only one lamination and only one groove; in Fig 4 it has two laminations and only one groove; in Fig 5 it has two laminations and one groove, the latter having been

rolled into one lamination as well as into the body of the closure.

Alternative embodiment

There are various possibilities with regard to the relative disposition of the sides which are grooved and the sides which are laminated, as illustrated in Fig 6, which presents end views along the longitudinal axis. Fig 6A shows a closure with lamination on one side only and with no groove; Fig 6B shows a closure with laminations on only one groove, both being on the same side; Fig 6D shows a closure with only one lamination and only one groove, both being on the same side and the groove having been rolled into the lamination as well as into the body of the closure; Fig 6E shows a closure with only one lamination and only one groove, the two being on opposite sides; Fig 6F shows a closure with two laminations and only one groove; Fig 6G shows a closure with two laminations and only one groove, the groove having been rolled into one lamination as well as into the body of the closure; Fig 6H shows a closure with only one lamination and with two grooves; Fig 6I shows a closure with only one lamination and with two grooves, one of the grooves having been rolled into the lamination as well as into the body of the closure; Fig 6J shows a closure with two laminations and with two grooves; Fig 6K shows a closure with two laminations and with two grooves, the grooves having been rolled into the laminations as well as into the body of the closure; and Fig 6L shows a closure with two laminations and a longitudinal through-hole.

Operation of Invention. Following a description of the invention, the specification includes an "operation" section that describes the action of the invention's parts. The operation section should not introduce any part that was not introduced in the description.

The manner of using the paper-laminated closure to seal a plastic bag is identical to that for closures in present use. Namely, one first twists the neck of a bag (not shown here but shown in Fig 12 of my above patent) into a narrow, cylindrical configuration. Next, holding the closure so that the plane of its base is generally perpendicular to the axis of the neck and so that lead-in notch 12 is adjacent to the neck, one inserts the twisted neck into the lead-in notch until it is forced past gripping points 16 at the base of the notch and into hole 14.

To remove the closure, one first bends it along its horizontal axis (Fig 1C—an end view—and Figs 7 and 8) so that the closure is still in contact with the neck of the bag and so that gripping points 16 roughly point in parallel directions. Then one pulls the closure up or down and away from the neck in a direction generally opposite to that in which the gripping points now point, thus freeing the closure from the bag without damaging the latter.

The presence of one or two grooves 18 or a longitudinal through-hole 26 (Fig 6L), either of which acts as a hinge, facilitates this process of bending.

The closure can be used to reseal the original bag or to seal another bag many times; one simply bends it flat again prior to reuse.

As shown in Figs 1C, 7B, and 8B (all end views), when the closure is bent along its longitudinal axis, region 30 of the base will stretch somewhat along the direction perpendicular to the longitudinal axis. (Region 30 is the region which is parallel to this axis and is on the side of the base opposite to the bend.) Therefore, when the closure is flattened again, the base will have elongated in the direction perpendicular to the longitudinal axis. This will cause a necking down 28 (Figs 1D, 7C, and 8C) of the base, as well as either a telltale tear 22, or at least a crease 32 (Figs 7A and 8A) along the axis of bending. Therefore, if the closure is attached to a sales item by a dishonest consumer from the first item to another will be made evident by the tear or crease.

Figs 7A and 8A show bent closures with and without grooves, respectively. Figs 7C and 8C show the same closures, respectively, after being flattened out, along their longitudinal axes, paper tear 22 being visible.

Conclusion, Ramifications, and Scope of Invention. The end of the operation section of the specification often provides a conclusion, summing up the invention, listing any additional ramifications that are not important enough to show in the drawing, and pointing the reader toward the patent claims.

The reader will see that the paper-laminated closure of this invention can be used to seal a plastic bag easily and conveniently. It can be removed just as easily and without damage to the bag. It can also be used to reseal the bag without requiring a new closure. In addition, when a closure has been used to seal a bag and is later bent and removed so as not to damage the bag, a tear or crease will appear in the paper lamination. This will create visible evidence of tampering without impairing the ability of the closure to reseal the original bag or any other bag. Furthermore, the paper lamination has the additional advantages in that:

(a) it permits the production of closures in a variety of colors without requiring the manufacturer to use a separate facility for the compounding of the powdered or liquid pigments needed for production

(b) it permits an immediate change in the color of the closure being produced without the need for purging the extruder of old resin

(c) it allows the closure to be brightly colored without the need to pigment the base itself and consequently sacrifice the flexibility of the closure. It also allows the closure to be multi-

colored since the paper lamination offers a perfect surface upon which can be printed multicolored designs

(d) it provides a closure with a superior surface upon which one can label or print

(e) it provides a closure whose labeling cannot be altered or erased without resulting in tell-tale damage to the paper lamination

(f) it provides a closure which will not be slippery when handled with wet or greasy fingers. The paper itself provides a nonslip surface.

Although the description above contains many specificities, these should not be of some of the presently preferred embodiments of this invention. For example, the closure can have other shapes, such as circular, oval, trapezoidal, triangular, etc.; the lead-in notch can have other shapes; the groove can be replaced by a hinge which connects two otherwise unconnected halves, etc.

Thus the scope of the invention should be determined by the appended claims and their legal equivalents, rather than by the examples given.

Computer Program. Computer programs having less than 60 lines will be provided in the Detailed Description. Those having from 60 to 300 lines may be provided in the drawing or here. If the program has over 300 lines, it will be provided on a compact disc.

12. Sequence Listing

If a biotech invention includes a sequence listing of a nucleotide or amino acid sequence, the applicant attaches this information on separate sheets of paper and references the sequence listing in the application (see PTO Rule 77). If there is no sequence listing, the applicant can omit this section or state, "non applicable."

D. Claims

Patent claims establish the boundaries or scope of an invention. They are the standard by which patent rights are measured. In other words, when a patent owner sues for infringement it is because someone has made, used, or sold an invention that has all of the elements in one of the claims, or that closely fits the description in the claims. In this manner, claims function like the boundaries in a deed for real estate. The claims are subject to rigorous examination during patent prosecution (the process of applying for a patent, see Chapter 6).

1. Claims Language

The patent claims must be specific enough to distinguish the invention from prior art. They must also be clear, logical, and precise (see 35 U.S.C. § 112(2)). Nonetheless, claims are often the hardest part of the patent to decipher. One reason is that claims follow strict grammatical requirements: they are sentence fragments, always start with an initial capital letter, and contain one period and no quotation marks or parentheses, except in mathematical or chemical formulas. The claims also contain obtuse terminology (see Section C2). To provide an idea of claims drafting, examples of claims for some common inventions and processes are provided below:

Claims for an Automobile:
A self-propelled vehicle, comprising:
  (a) a body carriage having rotatable wheels mounted thereunder for enabling said body carriage to roll along a surface
  (b) an engine mounted in said carriage for producing rotational energy, and
  (c) means for controllably coupling rotational energy from said engine to at least one of said wheels,
whereby said carriage can be self-propelled along said surface.

Claims for the Process of Sewing:
A method for joining two pieces of cloth together at their edges, comprising the steps of:
  (a) providing said two pieces of cloth and positioning them together so that an edge portion of one piece overlaps an adjacent edge portion of the other piece, and
  (b) passing a thread repeatedly through and along the length of the overlap-

ping portions in sequentially opposite directions and through sequentially spaced holes in said overlapping adjacent portions, whereby said two pieces of cloth will be attached along said edge portions.

Claims for Concrete:

A rigid building and paving material comprising a mixture of
  (a) sand and stones, and
  (b) a hardened cement binder filling the interstices between and adhering to sand and stones,
whereby a hardened, rigid, and strong matrix for building and paving will be provided.

Claims for a Pencil:

A hand-held writing instrument comprising:
  (a) elongated core-element means that will leave a marking line if moved across paper or other similar surface, and
  (b) an elongated holder surrounding and encasing said elongated core-element means, one portion of said holder being removable from an end thereof to expose an end of said core-element means so as to enable said core-element means to be exposed for writing,
whereby said holder protects said core-element means from breakage and provides an enlarged means for holding said core-element means conveniently.

Claims for the "Insert" Feature Of Word Processing:

A method of inserting additional characters within an existing series of characters on a display, comprising:
  (a) providing a memory which is able to store a series of characters at an adjacent series of addresses in said memory
  (b) providing a character input means which a human operator can use to store a series of characters in said memory at said respective adjacent series of addresses
  (c) storing said series of characters in said memory at said adjacent series of addresses
  (d) providing a display which is operatively connected to said memory for displaying said series of characters stored in said memory at said adjacent series of addresses
  (e) providing a pointer means which said operator can manipulate to point to any location between any adjacent characters within said series of characters displayed on said display
  (f) providing a memory controller which will
    (1) direct any additional character which said operator enters via said character input means to a location in said memory, beginning at an address corresponding to the location between said adjacent characters

as displayed on said display, and

(2) causing all characters in said series of characters which are stored in said memory at addresses subsequent said location in said memory to be transferred to subsequent addresses in said memory so that said additional character will be stored in said memory at said location and before all of said subsequent characters,

whereby said display will display said additional character within said series of characters at said location between said adjacent characters, and

whereby a writer can add words within existing body of text and the added words are displayed in an orderly and clean fashion without having to reenter said existing body of text.

In addition to Section 112, rules regarding the drafting of claims are provided in the PTO's "Rules of Practice." (PTO Rule 75, parts (b), (d)(1), and (e).)

2. Defining Common Terms

The following terms and their meanings may prove helpful in deciphering the arcane language of patent claims.

about (used when the applicant cannot provide a specific quantity) "The thread engagement is undone by rotating the lid unit *about* 90 degrees from the tightened position."

contiguous (used to indicate elements are touching) "Each slide-preventing stop has an upper end surface which is *contiguous* to one side edge of the upper end surface."

device for (interpreted as "means for") "It is an expansile *device for* use in blood vessels and tracts in the body and tension application *device for* use therewith and method."

disposed (used to indicate a part is positioned in a particular place) "A snap-action spring member is *disposed* in a cut portion formed in the outer lid."

further including (used in dependent claims to add additional parts) " … said lid unit *further including* a generally L-shaped spring member."

heretofore (used to refer back to something previously recited) "There have *heretofore* been strong user demands that such an indication should be provided on the top of the lid."

indicium (singular for indices; used to recite something that a human can recognize, such as a mark or a sound) " … so as to provide a field gradient operative to provide an *indicium* of the linear position of the shuttle."

means for (used to claim something broadly in terms of its function, rather than specific hardware) "It is an additional object of the invention to provide a compact *means for* pumping a medicament."

member (used to recite a mechanical part when no other word is available) " …

attached at one end to a drive *member* and at the other end to a fixed point on the base of the pump."

multitude (used to recite a large, indefinite number) "In addition, the programming time itself increases to accommodate the *multitude* of different programming thresholds."

pivotably (used to indicate that a part is rotatably mounted) "The blade is *pivotably* carried at one of its ends around a support shaft."

plurality (used to introduce more than one of an element) " ... a ROM memory having a *plurality* of reference potential transmission lines."

predetermined (used to state that a part has a specific parameter) "Programming stops when the gate threshold voltage has reached a certain *predetermined* point."

providing (used to recite a part in a method claim) "Oxide-nitride-oxide layers are formed above the channel area and between the bit lines for *providing* isolation between overlying polysilicon word lines."

respectively (used to relate several parts to several other parts in an individual manner) "A left and a right bit are stored in physically different areas of the charge trapping layer, near left and right regions of the memory cell, *respectively*."

said (used to refer to a previously recited part by exactly the same word) " ... *said* memory cell having a first region and a second region with a channel there between and having a gate above *said* channel."

sandwiching (used to indicate that one part is between two other parts) "Further, the thinner top and bottom oxide *sandwiching* the nitride layer helps in retention of the trapped charge."

slidably (used to indicate that two parts slide with respect to each other) "The charging roller bearing is *slidably* fitted in a guide groove."

so that (used to restrict a part to a defined function) "The cup holders are usually provided with annular grooves or vertical flutes *so that* the holder is only in contact with the cup."

substantially (used to fudge a specific recitation) "The side plate which has the hole is also provided with a toner filling opening *substantially* shaped like a right triangle."

such that (used to restrict a part to a defined function) "These grooves or flutes provide a structural integrity to the cup holders *such that* they must be packaged in substantially the same form as they will be used."

surrounding (used to indicate that a part is surrounded) "The elastic sealing members exactly cover the corresponding lengthwise end portions of the flange *surrounding* the recessed surface."

thereby (used to specify a result or connection between an element and what it does) "Said sleeping bag is supported by said carrying straps and carried *thereby* on one's back."

thereof (used as a pronoun to avoid repeating a part name) "Said back wall each being padded and being of equal width, being joined at the sides and the bottom *thereof*.

urging (used to indicate that force is exacted upon a part) "By pressing the rod against the *urging* of the spring, the link members straighten out."

whereby (used to introduce a function or result at the end of a claim) "*Whereby* the handle portion attaches to the handle of the device by the securing mechanisms."

wherein (used in a dependent claim to recite an element (part) more specifically) "A portable printing device as claimed in claim 13, *wherein* the shutter member includes ..."

3. Independent and Dependent Claims

Claims are usually made up of independent and dependent claims. One claim is stated as broadly as possible (the "independent claim") and then followed successively with narrower claims designed to specifically recite possible variations ("dependent claims"). The independent claim stands by itself while a dependent claim always refers back and incorporates the language of another independent or dependent claim (see 35 U.S.C. § 112(3) and (4)). Below is an example of an independent and dependent claim for a golf club and bag security system (Pat. No. 5,973,596). In this example, the independent claim defines the elements of the golf bag security system

and the dependent claim recites one aspect of it more specifically by stating that the alarm can be turned on and off by a separate device.

Independent Claim

1. *A golf bag security system for detecting movement of at least one golf club in a golf bag, the golf bag security system comprising:*
   a. *a detection loop substantially arranged around the circumference of a golf bag*
   b. *a loop oscillator circuit, connected to the detection loop*
   c. *a control circuit, capable of detecting a change in inductance in the loop, identifying an alarm condition in response to the change of inductance, and*
   d. *an alarm device responsive to the alarm condition.*

Dependent Claim

2. *The system defined in claim 1, additionally comprising an arming device enabling or disabling the security system.*

4. Reading Patent Claims for Infringement

In an infringement case, a court examines the claims of the patented invention and then compares them to the defendant's device or process. The court determines if the claims read on (or cover) the defendant's device or process. To infringe a patent, the defendant's device must physically have or perform all of the elements contained in one of the claims. For example, if a patent claim recites two elements, (1) a hidden pocket in a scarf, and (2) a snap that makes the pocket detachable, a device that contains only a hidden pocket in a scarf won't infringe.

A dependent claim cannot be infringed unless the allegedly infringing invention also infringes the related independent claim. In other words, if an independent claim is not infringed, then the dependent claims cannot be infringed.

E. Abstract

Although introduced relatively recently, the most widely read portion of the patent is the abstract. The abstract is a concise, one-paragraph summary of the structure, nature, and purpose of the entire disclosure. The abstract is used by the PTO and the public to quickly determine the gist of what is being disclosed. The abstract is really a condensed version of the specification (see Section B). Below are examples of two abstracts.

Abstract for Doll Carrier
(Pat. No. 5,803,331. See Fig. 5B, below)
ABSTRACT: A carrier for doll-type toys is provided having a pocket like enclosure for carrying the doll-type toy in a partially displayed position. The enclosure includes a double wall section forming an envelope or bag, in which the doll-type toy is carried, and a single wall section, against which the doll-type toy is partially displayed. This single wall section extends beyond and above the double walled section. Carrying straps permit the enclosure to be carried on the back of a child in backpack fashion. The carrying straps are attached adjacent to the free end of the single wall section and at the side of the double wall section. A second and smaller pocket enclosure may be attached to the front face of the carrier.

Abstract for Cup holder
(Pat. No. 5,425,497—Sold Under the
Trademark "Java Jacket." See Fig. 5C, be-
low)
A cup holder is disclosed in the form of a sheet with distal ends. A web is formed in one of the ends, and a corresponding slot is formed in the other end such that the ends interlock. Thus the cup holder is assembled by rolling the sheet and interlocking the ends. The sheet can be an elongate band of pressed material, preferably pressed paper pulp, and is preferably formed with multiple nubbins and depressions. In one embodiment, the sheet has a top and bottom that are accurate and concentric, and matching webs and cuts are formed in each end of the sheet, with the cuts being perpendicular to the top of the sheet.

Writing About Trademarks in Patents.
A trademark is any word or other symbol that is consistently associated with a product or service and identifies and distinguishes that product or service from others in the marketplace. If a patent applicant refers to a trademarked product, the trademark should be capitalized and used as an adjective (not a noun), followed by the generic name of the product or service, for example, *The Club* automobile anti-theft lock (not simply as *"The Club"*). When referring to the trademark, there should also be a reference to the trademark owner, for example, *"The Club* automobile anti-theft lock distributed by Winner International of Sharon, Pennsylvania."* (For more information on trademarks, see Chapter 1, Section H.)

F. Drawings

Patent drawings (also known as "drawing sheets") are visual representations of the invention and must be included with the application, if necessary, to understand the patent. The drawings must show every feature recited in the claims.

There are strict standards for patent drawings as to materials, size, form, symbols, and shading. For example, writing is not permitted in the margins and there can be no holes punched in the drawing sheet. A patent applicant has two choices when filing a patent: the application can include formal or informal drawings. Formal drawings are usually CAD drawings or other computer-created drawings, or copies of ink drawings done with instruments on bristol board or Mylar film and in accordance with PTO rules. Informal drawings are usually photocopies of good pencil or ink sketches which include all the details of the invention. Under a new rule (Rule 85), the application can be filed with informal drawings but will not be examined until formal drawings are filed. If an applicant wants to file abroad, formal drawings will usually have to be filed with the foreign application within 12 months after the patent application is filed. Also, formal drawings must be filed after the U.S. patent is allowed. For more information about patent drawing requirements, read *How to Make Patent Drawings Yourself,* by Patent Agent Jack Lo and Attorney David Pressman (Nolo), and see 35 U.S.C. § 113 and 37 CFR §§ 1.53 & 1.84.

The applicant may no longer use black-and-white photos for patent drawings unless a photo is necessary to show the invention—for example, fine structures such as a granular composition. Color photos or color drawings may also be used if necessary to illustrate the invention properly. In that case, an applicant must file three sets of color photos or drawings. A statement must be included in the specification referencing the colored drawings, and a petition explaining why color is necessary, along with a fee, must be filed. All drawings must be submitted in either 8½ x 11 inch size (U.S. standard) or 210 mm x 297 mm size (A4 international standard).

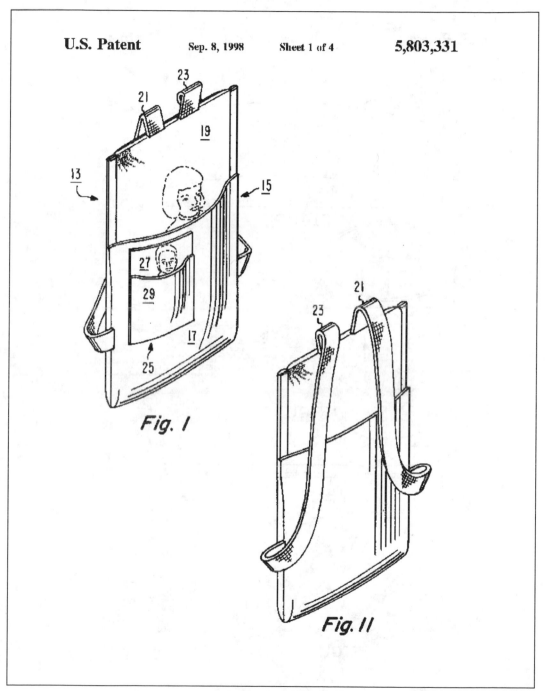

Fig. I

Fig. II

Figure 5B—Doll Carrier

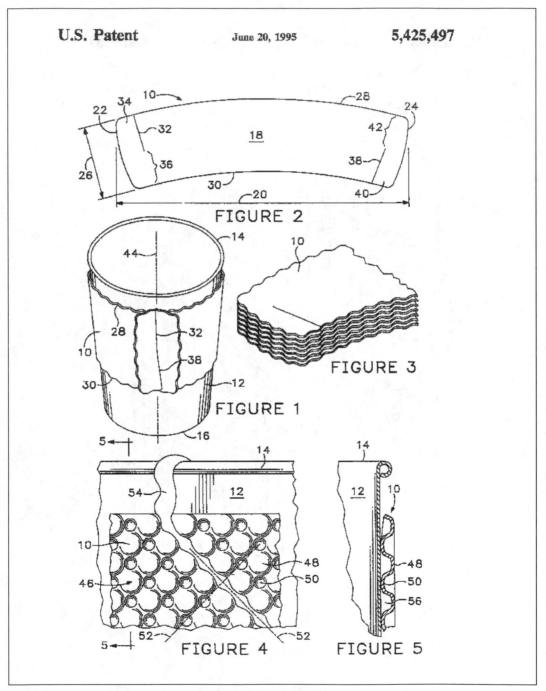

Figure 5C—Cupholder

G. Preparation of a Patent Application

In this section, we provide basic information about a patent application. For detailed information on preparing a patent application, read *Patent It Yourself*, by patent attorney David Pressman (Nolo).

The preparation of a patent application requires assembling a group of documents according to PTO rules. Below is a table of documents used for patent application preparation.

1. Specification, Claims, Abstract, and Drawings

These documents make up the substance of the patent application and are discussed in detail in Sections B, C, D, and E, respectively.

2. Information Disclosure Statement

The PTO rules impose on each patent applicant a "duty of candor and good faith." This means that all applicants and their attorneys must disclose information about prior art they are aware of that might influence the patent examiner in deciding on the application. The Information Disclosure Statement (IDS) is used to comply with this candor requirement. All applicants must submit an IDS at the time of filing the application, within the following three months, or before the First Office Action. (For information on office actions, see Chapter 6). The IDS consists of a transmittal letter and a "PTO Form SB/08," on which prior art is listed. An example of a completed IDS is shown in Figs. 5D and 5E, below. An applicant who is not aware of any relevant prior art does not have to file an IDS. An applicant who later becomes aware of relevant prior art must disclose it by a later IDS. A fee must be paid if the IDS is filed after the First Office Action.

The applicant must also include with the IDS a copy of each cited reference and a discussion of the relevance of any non-English language references to the invention. In other words copies of articles and patents must be attached. You may wonder why an applicant has to send patents to the PTO, the repository of the nation's patent collection. The PTO maintains that it's such a large and complex organization that it would cause too many administrative difficulties and require too much of the examiners' time to locate the patents cited by applicants.

3. Patent Application Declaration (PAD)

The declaration identifies the inventor or joint inventors and provides a statement by the applicant that the inventor understands

Documents Used for Patent Application Preparation

Specification	Required (see Section B).
Claims	Required (see Section C).
Abstract	Required (see Section D).
Drawings	Required if necessary to understand the invention (see Section E).
Information Disclosure Statement	Required if applicant knows of any relevant prior art, but can be filed within 3 months of application (see Section F2).
Patent Application Declaration (PAD)	Required (see Section F3).
Petition to Make Special	Optional and can be filed at any time (see Section F6).
Assignment and Cover Sheet	Required if an inventor is transferring ownership of patent. Can be filed at any time (see Section F7).
Disclosure Document Reference Letter	Required if a Disclosure Document was filed previously (see Section F8).
Return Receipt Postcard (optional)	Optional, but desirable (see Section F9).
Filing Fee	Required (see Section F10).
Transmittal Letter	Required.*
Fee Transmittal	Required.*
Credit Card Payment Form	Required.*

*Although not strictly required, the transmittal letter and fee transmittal are usually included. For more information on the technical details regarding transmittal letters and fee transmittals, review PTO Rules at the PTO website, www.uspto.gov.

the contents of the claims and specification and has fully disclosed all material information. The PTO provides a form for the declaration (see Fig. 5F). (For more information, see 35 U.S.C. § 115 and 37 CFR §§ 1.51–1.68.)

4. Power of Attorney

Only an inventor, a patent agent, or a patent attorney may prepare and file a patent application. If an attorney is preparing an application on behalf of an inventor, a power of attorney should be executed to authorize the patent attorney or agent to act on behalf of the inventor. The power of attorney form is usually part of the PAD. If the rights to the patent have been assigned and the assignment has been recorded, the assignee can execute the power of attorney. If the inventor is preparing and filing the application "pro se" (without an attorney), then a power of attorney is not necessary. (See 37 CFR § 1.34.)

5. Small Entity (Fees)

In order to encourage inventors from diverse economic backgrounds, fees are reduced for small businesses, independent inventors, and nonprofit companies. An independent inventor must either own all rights, or have transferred—or be obligated to transfer—rights to a small business or nonprofit organization. Nonprofit organizations are defined and listed in the Code of Federal Regulations and usually are educational institutions or charitable organizations. A small entity business is one with less than 500 employees. The number of employees is computed by averaging the number of full- and part-time employees during a fiscal year.

If the inventor qualifies as a small entity, a Small Entitiy Declaration is no longer required. The inventor simply indicates that he or she is entitled to small entity status on the Fee Transmittal and pays the small entity fee. Small entity status is lost if patent rights are transferred—or obligated to be transferred—to an entity that does not qualify as a small entity. In that case the inventor is obligated to tell the PTO that small entity status is no longer appropriate and the inventor must pay large entity fees after that.

6. Petition to Make Special

An applicant can, under certain circumstances, have an application examined sooner than the normal course of PTO examination, which is usually one to two years. This is accomplished by filing a "Petition to Make Special" (PTMS), together with a Supporting Declaration. This can be filed with the application or at any time after. As a general rule, most patent professionals agree that the PTMS is of little value

In the United States Patent and Trademark Office

Serial Number: _____

Appn. Filed: _____

Applicant(s): _____

Appn. Title: _____

Examiner/GAU: _____

Mailed: _____

At: _____

Information Disclosure Statement

Assistant Commissioner for Patents

Washington, District of Columbia 20231

Sir:

Attached is a completed Form PTO-1449 and copies of the pertinent parts of the references cited thereon. Following are comments on any non-English-language references pursuant to Rule 98:

Very respectfully,

Applicant(s): _____

_____

Enc.: PTO-1449 & References

c/o: _____

_____

_____

Telephone: _____

Certificate of Mailing

I certify that this correspondence will be deposited with the United States Postal Service as first class mail with proper postage affixed in an envelope addressed to: "Assistant Commissioner for Patents, Washington, DC 20231" on the date below.

Date: 200 _____   _____

Figure 5D—Information Disclosure Statement

PTO/SB/08A (10-01)
Approved for use through 10/31/2002. OMB 0651-0031
U.S. Patent and Trademark Office: U.S. DEPARTMENT OF COMMERCE
Under the Paperwork Reduction Act of 1995, no persons are required to respond to a collection of information unless it contains a valid OMB control number.

Substitute for form 1449A/PTO

INFORMATION DISCLOSURE STATEMENT BY APPLICANT

(use as many sheets as necessary)

Sheet		of	

Complete if Known

Application Number	
Filing Date	
First Named Inventor	
Art Unit	
Examiner Name	
Attorney Docket Number	

U.S. PATENT DOCUMENTS

Examiner Initials*	Cite No.[1]	Document Number — Number - Kind Code[2] (if known)	Publication Date MM-DD-YYYY	Name of Patentee or Applicant of Cited Document	Pages, Columns, Lines, Where Relevant Passages or Relevant Figures Appear
		US-			
		US-			
		US-			
		US-			
		US-			
		US-			
		US-			
		US-			
		US-			
		US-			
		US-			
		US-			
		US-			
		US-			
		US-			
		US-			
		US-			
		US-			
		US-			
		US-			

FOREIGN PATENT DOCUMENTS

Examiner Initials*	Cite No.[1]	Foreign Patent Document — Country Code[3] -Number[4] - Kind Code[5] (if known)	Publication Date MM-DD-YYYY	Name of Patentee or Applicant of Cited Document	Pages, Columns, Lines, Where Relevant Passages or Relevant Figures Appear	T[6]

Examiner Signature		Date Considered	

*EXAMINER: Initial if reference considered, whether or not citation is in conformance with MPEP 609. Draw line through citation if not in conformance and not considered. Include copy of this form with next communication to applicant.

[1] Applicant's unique citation designation number (optional). [2] See Kinds Codes of USPTO Patent Documents at www.uspto.gov or MPEP 901.04. [3] Enter Office that issued the document, by the two-letter code (WIPO Standard ST.3). [4] For Japanese patent documents, the indication of the year of the reign of the Emperor must precede the serial number of the patent document. [5] Kind of document by the appropriate symbols as indicated on the document under WIPO Standard ST. 16 if possible. [6] Applicant is to place a check mark here if English language Translation is attached.

Burden Hour Statement: This form is estimated to take 2.0 hours to complete. Time will vary depending upon the needs of the individual case. Any comments on the amount of time you are required to complete this form should be sent to the Chief Information Officer, U.S. Patent and Trademark Office, Washington, DC 20231. DO NOT SEND FEES OR COMPLETED FORMS TO THIS ADDRESS. SEND TO: Assistant Commissioner for Patents, Washington, DC 20231.

Figure 5E—PTO Form SB/08

PTO/SB/01 (10-01)
Approved for use through 10/31/2002. OMB 0651-0032
U.S. Patent and Trademark Office; U.S. DEPARTMENT OF COMMERCE
Under the Paperwork Reduction Act of 1995, no persons are required to respond to a collection of information unless it contains a valid OMB control number.

DECLARATION FOR UTILITY OR DESIGN PATENT APPLICATION (37 CFR 1.63)	Attorney Docket Number	
	First Named Inventor	
	COMPLETE IF KNOWN	
	Application Number	
☐ Declaration Submitted with Initial Filing **OR** ☐ Declaration Submitted after Initial Filing (surcharge (37 CFR 1.16 (e)) required)	Filing Date	
	Art Unit	
	Examiner Name	

As the below named inventor, I hereby declare that:

My residence, mailing address, and citizenship are as stated below next to my name.

I believe I am the original and first inventor of the subject matter which is claimed and for which a patent is sought on the invention entitled:

(Title of the Invention)

the specification of which

☐ is attached hereto

OR

☐ was filed on (MM/DD/YYYY) _____ as United States Application Number or PCT International

Application Number _____ and was amended on (MM/DD/YYYY) _____ (if applicable).

I hereby state that I have reviewed and understand the contents of the above identified specification, including the claims, as amended by any amendment specifically referred to above.

I acknowledge the duty to disclose information which is material to patentability as defined in 37 CFR 1.56, including for continuation-in-part applications, material information which became available between the filing date of the prior application and the national or PCT international filing date of the continuation-in-part application.

I hereby claim foreign priority benefits under 35 U.S.C. 119(a)-(d) or (f), or 365(b) of any foreign application(s) for patent, inventor's or plant breeder's rights certificate(s), or 365(a) of any PCT international application which designated at least one country other than the United States of America, listed below and have also identified below, by checking the box, any foreign application for patent, inventor's or plant breeder's rights certificate(s), or any PCT international application having a filing date before that of the application on which priority is claimed.

Prior Foreign Application Number(s)	Country	Foreign Filing Date (MM/DD/YYYY)	Priority Not Claimed	Certified Copy Attached? YES	NO
			☐	☐	☐
			☐	☐	☐
			☐	☐	☐
			☐	☐	☐

☐ Additional foreign application numbers are listed on a supplemental priority data sheet PTO/SB/02B attached hereto:

[Page 1 of 2]

Burden Hour Statement: This form is estimated to take 21 minutes to complete. Time will vary depending upon the needs of the individual case. Any comments on the amount of time you are required to complete this form should be sent to the Chief Information Officer, U.S. Patent and Trademark Office, Washington, DC 20231. DO NOT SEND FEES OR COMPLETED FORMS TO THIS ADDRESS. SEND TO: Assistant Commissioner for Patents, Washington, DC 20231.

Figure 5F—Patent Application Declaration

since it usually advances the examination only a few months. The standards for filing a PTMS are listed below. A petition fee must be paid if filing a PTMS, unless the petition is for reasons 3–6 or 9.

1. Manufacturer Available. A manufacturer is available—that is, a person or company exists that will manufacture the invention provided the patent application is allowed or a patent issues.

2. Infringement Exists. Someone is making, using, or selling the invention covered by the patent application and the applicant needs a patent to sue the infringer or get the infringer to pay royalties.

3. Applicant's Health Is Poor. The applicant's life span has been shortened by poor health.

4. Applicant's Age Is 65 or Greater.

5. Environmental Quality Will Be Enhanced.

6. Energy Savings Will Result.

7. Recombinant DNA Is Involved.

8. Search Was Made. If the applicant has made a search and submitted an Information Disclosure Statement—as required anyway (see Section F2 above)—the applicant can get the case made special.

9. Superconductivity Is Advanced. Public policy favors the exploitation of this scientific phenomenon.

10. Relates to HIV/AIDS or Cancer.

11. Counters Terrorism.

A form for the PTMS is available at the PTO website, www.uspto.gov, or Form 10-7 from *Patent It Yourself,* by David Pressman (Nolo), can be used.

7. Assignment

A patent application must be filed in the name of the true inventor or inventors. If there is more than one inventor, each becomes an applicant for the patent and each automatically owns equal shares of the invention and any patents that may issue. (For more information about patent ownership, see Chapter 7, Section C.)

Inventorship can be different from ownership. Often all or part of the ownership of the invention and the patent application must be transferred to someone else or some business entity. For example, the inventor may work for a company and as a condition of employment, has agreed to transfer ownership of inventions. To make the transfer, the inventor must legally transfer the interest by assignment. This is accomplished as follows: the application is filed in the name of the inventor and the assignment is also filed either with the patent application or at any time afterward. Some inventors prefer to wait until they have a received a serial number for the application before filing the assignment.

If an assignment of a patent application has been recorded and the applicant refers to that fact in the issue fee transmittal form (see Section F11), the PTO will print the patent with the assignee's interest indicated. For example, an egg storage device patent was assigned and the inventor and assignee were listed as follows:

> *INVENTOR: Onneweer, Frederik J.,*
> *Tervuren, Belgium*
> *ASSIGNEE AT ISSUE: Dart Industries Inc.,*
> *Deerfield, Illinois*

Even if the patent doesn't indicate the assignment, the assignment will still be effective if the PTO has recorded it. The PTO currently charges $40 to record an assignment and requires that all assignments submitted for recording be accompanied by a cover letter.

8. Disclosure Document Reference Letter

If the applicant previously filed a disclosure document referencing the invention and its prior art (see Chapter 3, Section D), then a Disclosure Document Reference Letter (DDRL) should be enclosed with the application. This short letter provides the title, number, and filing date of the previously filed disclosure document. The filing of a DDRL will alert the PTO to retain the disclosure document. Otherwise, the PTO will dispose of the disclosure document after two years.

9. Return Receipt Postcard

Since it often takes months for the PTO to officially acknowledge receipt of an application or any other paper, the only way to quickly verify receipt is to enclose a stamped return postcard with the mailed materials. The back of the card contains the inventor's name, title of invention, number of pages of specification, claims, abstract, the date the Patent Application Declaration was signed, the number of sheets of drawing (and whether formal or informal), the Small Entity Declaration, and the check number and amount. The applicant usually receives the postcard back from the PTO within two to four weeks of filing the application.

10. Check, Money Order or Credit Card Payment for Correct Filing Fee

The applicant must enclose the appropriate fee, a Fee Transmittal Letter (see Fig. 5G, below) and a Credit Card Payment Form (if paying by the credit card). The fee depends on several variables, including the number of independent and dependent claims, whether the applicant qualifies for Small Entity Status (see Section F5, above), and whether an assignment is being filed (see Section F7, above). Payment can be made by personal check or money order made out to the *Commissioner of Patents and*

Trademarks for the total amount, and should be attached to the transmittal letter. The PTO also accepts payment by credit card. An applicant paying by credit card must use the PTO's Credit Card Payment Form (PTO Form 2038) with the Fee Transmittal. The PTO does not accept debit cards or check cards requiring a personal identification number (PIN).

11. Transmittal Letter

The transmittal letter is the cover letter that details what is being filed, the names of inventors, the number of pages, the fee, and other information used by the PTO to categorize the filing (see Fig. 5H, below). If the applicant previously filed a Disclosure Document or a provisional patent application, that information should also be listed. The transmittal letter also permits an inventor to ask the examiner to write allowable claims for the invention. (See MPEP § 707.07(j).) All of the inventors must sign the transmittal letter. The entire package of application materials is mailed to: Box Patent Application, Commissioner for Patents, Washington, DC 20231. In Chapter 6,

we discuss what happens at the PTO after the application is filed.

Inventors can use form PTO-2038 to pay fees by credit card. The form can be downloaded from the PTO website.

Under new legislation all patent applications are published 18 months after filing unless at the time of filing, the inventor files a Non-Publication Request (PTO Form SB/35), stating that that the application will not be filed outside the U.S. If an inventor does not request non-publication the application will be published afer 18 months and the inventor will be charged $300 more when the application is allowed. If an inventor requests non-publication and subsequently files a foreign application, he or she must notify the PTO within 45 days and authorize publication.

 Electronic Filing. The PTO now provides software that enables applicants to file patent applications and provisional patent applications via the Internet. The PTO's Electronic Filing System (EFS) assembles application components (including figures), calculates fees and transits the completed application to the PTO via a digitally encrypted secure system.

PTO/SB/17 (11-01)
Approved for use through 10/31/2002. OMB 0651-0032
U.S. Patent and Trademark Office; U.S. DEPARTMENT OF COMMERCE
Under the Paperwork Reduction Act of 1995, no persons are required to respond to a collection of information unless it displays a valid OMB control number.

FEE TRANSMITTAL
for FY 2002
Patent fees are subject to annual revision.

☐ Applicant claims small entity status. See 37 CFR 1.27

TOTAL AMOUNT OF PAYMENT   ($)

Complete if Known

Application Number	
Filing Date	
First Named Inventor	
Examiner Name	
Group Art Unit	
Attorney Docket No.	

METHOD OF PAYMENT *(check all that apply)*

☐ Check ☐ Credit card ☐ Money Order ☐ Other ☐ None

☐ Deposit Account:

Deposit Account Number

Deposit Account Name

The Commissioner is authorized to: *(check all that apply)*

☐ Charge fee(s) indicated below   ☐ Credit any overpayments
☐ Charge any additional fee(s) during the pendency of this application
☐ Charge fee(s) indicated below, **except for the filing fee**
to the above-identified deposit account.

FEE CALCULATION

1. BASIC FILING FEE

Large Entity		Small Entity			
Fee Code	Fee ($)	Fee Code	Fee ($)	Fee Description	Fee Paid
101	740	201	370	Utility filing fee	
106	330	206	165	Design filing fee	
107	510	207	255	Plant filing fee	
108	740	208	370	Reissue filing fee	
114	160	214	80	Provisional filing fee	

SUBTOTAL (1) ($)

2. EXTRA CLAIM FEES FOR UTILITY AND REISSUE

	Extra Claims	Fee from below	Fee Paid
Total Claims	-20** =	X	=
Independent Claims	-3** =	X	=
Multiple Dependent		=	

Large Entity		Small Entity			
Fee Code	Fee ($)	Fee Code	Fee ($)	Fee Description	
103	18	203	9	Claims in excess of 20	
102	84	202	42	Independent claims in excess of 3	
104	280	204	140	Multiple dependent claim, if not paid	
109	84	209	42	** Reissue independent claims over original patent	
110	18	210	9	** Reissue claims in excess of 20 and over original patent	

SUBTOTAL (2) ($)

**or number previously paid, if greater; For Reissues, see above

FEE CALCULATION (continued)

3. ADDITIONAL FEES

Large Entity		Small Entity			
Fee Code	Fee ($)	Fee Code	Fee ($)	Fee Description	Fee Paid
105	130	205	65	Surcharge - late filing fee or oath	
127	50	227	25	Surcharge - late provisional filing fee or cover sheet	
139	130	139	130	Non-English specification	
147	2,520	147	2,520	For filing a request for *ex parte* reexamination	
112	920*	112	920*	Requesting publication of SIR prior to Examiner action	
113	1,840*	113	1,840*	Requesting publication of SIR after Examiner action	
115	110	215	55	Extension for reply within first month	
116	400	216	200	Extension for reply within second month	
117	920	217	460	Extension for reply within third month	
118	1,440	218	720	Extension for reply within fourth month	
128	1,960	228	980	Extension for reply within fifth month	
119	320	219	160	Notice of Appeal	
120	320	220	160	Filing a brief in support of an appeal	
121	280	221	140	Request for oral hearing	
138	1,510	138	1,510	Petition to institute a public use proceeding	
140	110	240	55	Petition to revive - unavoidable	
141	1,280	241	640	Petition to revive - unintentional	
142	1,280	242	640	Utility issue fee (or reissue)	
143	460	243	230	Design issue fee	
144	620	244	310	Plant issue fee	
122	130	122	130	Petitions to the Commissioner	
123	50	123	50	Processing fee under 37 CFR 1.17(q)	
126	180	126	180	Submission of Information Disclosure Stmt	
581	40	581	40	Recording each patent assignment per property (times number of properties)	
146	740	246	370	Filing a submission after final rejection (37 CFR § 1.129(a))	
149	740	249	370	For each additional invention to be examined (37 CFR § 1.129(b))	
179	740	279	370	Request for Continued Examination (RCE)	
169	900	169	900	Request for expedited examination of a design application	

Other fee (specify) _____

*Reduced by Basic Filing Fee Paid   **SUBTOTAL (3)** ($)

SUBMITTED BY			Complete *(if applicable)*	
Name *(Print/Type)*		Registration No. *(Attorney/Agent)*	Telephone	
Signature			Date	

WARNING: Information on this form may become public. Credit card information should not be included on this form. Provide credit card information and authorization on PTO-2038.

Burden Hour Statement: This form is estimated to take 0.2 hours to complete. Time will vary depending upon the needs of the individual case. Any comments on the amount of time you are required to complete this form should be sent to the Chief Information Officer, U.S. Patent and Trademark Office, Washington, DC 20231. DO NOT SEND FEES OR COMPLETED FORMS TO THIS ADDRESS. SEND TO: Assistant Commissioner for Patents, Washington, DC 20231.

Figure 5G—Fee Transmittal Letter

PTO/SB/05 (03-01)
Approved for use through 10/31/2002. OMB 0651-0032
U.S. Patent and Trademark Office; U.S. DEPARTMENT OF COMMERCE
Under the Paperwork Reduction Act of 1995, no persons are required to respond to a collection of information unless it displays a valid OMB control number.

Please type a plus sign (+) inside this box ➝ ☐

UTILITY
PATENT APPLICATION
TRANSMITTAL

(Only for new nonprovisional applications under 37 CFR 1.53(b))

Attorney Docket No.	
First Inventor	
Title	
Express Mail Label No.	

APPLICATION ELEMENTS

See MPEP chapter 600 concerning utility patent application contents.

1. ☐ Fee Transmittal Form (e.g., PTO/SB/17)
   (Submit an original and a duplicate for fee processing)

2. ☐ Applicant claims small entity status.
   See 37 CFR 1.27.

3. ☐ Specification   [Total Pages ☐]
   (preferred arrangement set forth below)
   - Descriptive title of the invention
   - Cross Reference to Related Applications
   - Statement Regarding Fed sponsored R & D
   - Reference to sequence listing, a table,
     or a computer program listing appendix
   - Background of the Invention
   - Brief Summary of the Invention
   - Brief Description of the Drawings *(if filed)*
   - Detailed Description
   - Claim(s)
   - Abstract of the Disclosure

4. ☐ Drawing(s) (35 U.S.C. 113)   [Total Sheets ☐]

5. Oath or Declaration   [Total Pages ☐]

   a. ☐ Newly executed (original or copy)
   b. ☐ Copy from a prior application (37 CFR 1.63 (d))
      (for continuation/divisional with Box 18 completed)

   i. ☐ **DELETION OF INVENTOR(S)**
      Signed statement attached deleting inventor(s)
      named in the prior application, see 37 CFR
      1.63(d)(2) and 1.33(b).

6. ☐ Application Data Sheet. See 37 CFR 1.76

ADDRESS TO:
Assistant Commissioner for Patents
Box Patent Application
Washington, DC 20231

7. ☐ CD-ROM or CD-R in duplicate, large table or
   Computer Program (*Appendix*)

8. Nucleotide and/or Amino Acid Sequence Submission
   (if applicable, all necessary)
   a. ☐ Computer Readable Form (CRF)
   b. Specification Sequence Listing on:
      i. ☐ CD-ROM or CD-R (2 copies); or
      ii. ☐ paper
   c. ☐ Statements verifying identity of above copies

ACCOMPANYING APPLICATION PARTS

9. ☐ Assignment Papers (cover sheet & document(s))
10. ☐ 37 CFR 3.73(b) Statement   ☐ Power of
    (when there is an assignee)   Attorney
11. ☐ English Translation Document *(if applicable)*
12. ☐ Information Disclosure   ☐ Copies of IDS
    Statement (IDS)/PTO-1449   Citations
13. ☐ Preliminary Amendment
14. ☐ Return Receipt Postcard (MPEP 503)
    (Should be specifically itemized)
15. ☐ Certified Copy of Priority Document(s)
    (if foreign priority is claimed)
16. ☐ Nonpublication Request under 35 U.S.C. 122
    (b)(2)(B)(i). Applicant must attach form PTO/SB/35
    or its equivalent.
17. ☐ Other: ....

18. If a CONTINUING APPLICATION, *check appropriate box, and supply the requisite information below and in a preliminary amendment,*
or *in an Application Data Sheet under 37 CFR 1.76:*

☐ Continuation   ☐ Divisional   ☐ Continuation-in-part (CIP)   of prior application No.: _____ / _____

Prior application information: Examiner _____   Group Art Unit: _____

For **CONTINUATION OR DIVISIONAL APPS** only: The entire disclosure of the prior application, from which an oath or declaration is supplied under Box 5b, is considered a part of the disclosure of the accompanying continuation or divisional application and is hereby incorporated by reference. The incorporation **can only** be relied upon when a portion has been inadvertently omitted from the submitted application parts.

19. CORRESPONDENCE ADDRESS

☐ Customer Number or Bar Code Label   [Insert Customer No. or Attach bar code label here]   or   ☐ Correspondence address below

Name	
Address	
City		State		Zip Code	
Country		Telephone		Fax	

| Name (Print/Type) | | Registration No. (Attorney/Agent) | |
| Signature | | Date | |

Burden Hour Statement: This form is estimated to take 0.2 hours to complete. Time will vary depending upon the needs of the individual case. Any comments on the amount of time you are required to complete this form should be sent to the Chief Information Officer, U.S. Patent and Trademark Office, Washington, DC 20231. DO NOT SEND FEES OR COMPLETED FORMS TO THIS ADDRESS. SEND TO: Assistant Commissioner for Patents, Box Patent Application, Washington, DC 20231.

Figure 5H—Patent Transmittal Letter

Chapter 6

Patent Prosecution and the PTO

cquiring a patent is a little like playing a board game. If you are the applicant, you must move the invention through the PTO examination process, avoiding certain obstacles, such as technical errors or delays, while preserving the strongest possible claims for patent protection. The process of shepherding a patent application through the PTO is known as patent prosecution. In this chapter, we discuss the common elements of patent prosecution and provide background on PTO procedures.

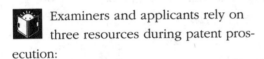 Examiners and applicants rely on three resources during patent prosecution:

- **Patent statutes.** The patent laws passed by Congress are found in Title 35 of the United States Code (35 U.S.C.)
- **Patent Rules of Practice.** The Patent Rules of Practice are administrative regulations located in Volume 37 of the Code of Federal Regulations (37 C.F.R. § 1), and
- *Manual of Patent Examining Procedure* **(MPEP).** The MPEP is often referred to as the "examiner's bible" because it covers almost any situation encountered in patent prosecution. It contains the PTO's Rules of Practice and the patent statutes described below.

These resources can be obtained from the PTO's Internet site, www.uspto.gov, and the CASSIS CD-ROMs at any PTDL. The PTO Rules of Practice and the patent statutes can also be found at regional government bookstores in paperbound form. Look in your local phone directory for the government bookstore nearest you.

Patent Prosecution and Foreign Filing. Filing a U.S. patent application has an impact on the ability to obtain a patent in foreign countries. After an application is filed in the U.S., an applicant may publish articles on the invention without loss of legal rights in the U.S. or in Convention countries (countries with which the U.S. has patent treaties) since the applicant will get the benefit of the U.S. filing date in all Convention countries. However, an applicant is not entitled to priority rights in the few remaining non-Convention countries, so the invention should not be published before actual filing in these countries. (For a list of Convention countries and information on international patent treaties and the relationship between U.S. and foreign filing, consult Chapter 9.)

A. Patent Prosecution: The Road to Allowance

Patent prosecution usually proceeds through the following steps:
- The PTO receives and catalogs the patent application

- A PTO examiner examines and initially rejects (or sometimes "allows," that is, "accepts") the claims of the application
- The applicant responds to the rejection with an amendment, and
- The PTO examiner reviews the amendment and either issues a Notice of Allowance or makes a final rejection of the application.

The goal during patent prosecution is to obtain a Notice of Allowance, a statement from a PTO examiner that the application meets the legal requirements of patentability. Of course, not all applications meet this standard. In the event the examiner sends a "final office action," there are still several options as discussed in Section B.

1. Receipt of Application

If a return postcard is enclosed with an application, the PTO will stamp and return this and it becomes the first correspondence from the PTO (see Chapter 5, Section F9). The postcard usually arrives within two to four weeks of filing. It is stamped with a date and an eight-digit number, for example, "U.S. Patent & TM Office, 22 August 2002; 09/801,666." The date is the "deposit" date, or date of receipt, and the number is the serial number (sometimes called "application number") of the inventor's application. The serial number and filing date should be maintained in confidence.

Within one to three months after mailing the application, the PTO sends an official filing receipt. The filing receipt contains more detailed information, such as the name(s) of the inventor(s), the title of the patent application, the examining group to which the application has been assigned, the filing date and serial number of the application, and the number of claims (total and independent). This information is entered into the PTO's data-processing system. If the filing receipt has any errors, these should be corrected by sending or faxing a brief letter to the Application Branch of the PTO.

Once the official filing receipt is mailed, the patent application is officially pending. At this point the invention and any descriptive literature can be labeled either as "Patent Pending" or "Patent Applied For" (both expressions mean the same thing, see sidebar below—Patent Pending Status).

If an administrative error was made in the application, such as failing to sign a form or pay the fee, the PTO's Application Branch will send a deficiency notice explaining what's required and sometimes also requiring a penalty fee. Once the applicant complies, the PTO will mail the filing receipt.

Filing the IDS. An Information Disclosure Statement (IDS) (see Chapter 5, Section F2) must be filed within three months of the application filing date.

Patent Extensions: When the PTO Takes Too Long

As a result of a law passed in 1999 (35 U.S.C. § 154(b)), the term of a patent will be extended for as long as necessary to compensate for any of the following:

- any delay caused by the PTO failing to examine a new application within 14 months from filing
- any delay caused by the PTO failing to take any of the following actions within four months:
  - reply to an amendment or to an appeal brief
  - issue an allowance or office action after a decision on appeal
  - issue a patent after the issue fee is paid and any required drawings are filed
- any delay caused by the PTO failing to issue a patent within three years from filing, unless the delay was due to the applicant filing a continuation or divisional application, or buying a delay to reply to an Office Action, or
- any delay due to secrecy orders, appeals or interferences.

Patent Pending Status

As explained in Chapter 1, an inventor has no patent rights until the patent actually issues. In other words, an invention that states "patent pending" can be copied freely by anyone. The purpose of marking a device patent pending is to give notice to potential infringers. Most potential infringers won't copy a patent pending device fearing that a patent will later issue and the money spent on expensive tooling would have been wasted. Although you cannot sue for patent infringement, it is possible to recover for infringements during the pendency period provided that the application is published under the 18-month rule (see below), issues as a patent and the infringer had notice during the pendency period.

It's a criminal offense to use the words "patent applied for" or "patent pending" in any advertising when there's no active, applicable regular or provisional patent application on file.

Publication of Pending Applications. As a result of legislation passed in 1999, every pending application will be published for the public to view 18 months after its earliest effective filing date, or earlier if requested. Moreover, if at the time of filing the applicant states that the application will not be filed abroad, the application will not be published. If the applicant later files the application abroad, the applicant must notify the PTO and authorize publication within 45 days.

The public will not be allowed to oppose or protest against any published application without the applicant's consent. An applicant whose application is published may obtain royalties from an infringer from the date of publication if the application later issues as a patent, provided the infringer had actual notice of the published application. The PTO is expected to charge a separate fee for publishing an application and this fee (to be posted at the PTO website) will be due after a notice of allowance is given. (35 USC §§ 122, 154.)

2. First Office Action

Within six months to two years after the filing date, the applicant will receive correspondence from the PTO known as a "first office action" (sometimes called an "official letter" or "OA"). You can determine an approximate date when the PTO will send the first office action by looking in a recent *Official Gazette* under "Examining Corps." Look for the appropriate examining group. Also you can call the clerk of the examining group. The *Official Gazette* and PTO phone numbers are available on the PTO's website, www.uspto.gov.

The first office action may:

- cite and enclose copies of prior art that the examiner believes shows the applicant's invention is obvious or lacks novelty

- reject claims
- list defects in the specification or drawings, or
- raise other objections.

It is very rare that an application is allowed in the first office action. More often, the examiner rejects some or all of the claims. Some examiners make a "shotgun" or "shoot-from-the-hip" rejection, flatly rejecting all claims for questionable reasons. Examiners sometimes do this because of the time pressures of work at the PTO or sometimes to force the applicant to state more clearly the essence of the invention and its distinguishing features.

An example of an office action is provided in Fig 6A. The first page of the OA details the examiner's objections to the application. The rule or law that is the basis for each objection is provided on pages 2 and 3 of the OA. The objections include:

1. The drawing is not complete because it fails to show certain features that are recited in the claims. This objection is based on Patent Rule 1.83(a).

2. The specification is inadequate because it does not demonstrate in sufficient detail how to make and use the invention. This rejection is based on Patent Rule 1.71(b).

3. Since the specification is inadequate, the examiner rejects all claims because the claims are based on an inadequate specification. This objection is based on Section 112 of the patent laws (35 U.S.C. § 112).

UNITED STATES DEPARTMENT OF COMMERCE
Patent and Trademark Office

Address : COMMISSIONER OF PATENTS AND TRADEMARKS
Washington, D.C. 20231

SERIAL NUMBER	FILING DATE	FIRST NAMED APPLICANT	ATTORNEY DOCKET NO.
07/345,678	1998 Aug 9	LeRoy Inventor	

Portia Barrister
1237 Chancery Lane
Puyallup, WA 98371-3841

Received 1998 Oct 14 P.B.

	EXAMINER
	HEYMAN, J
ART UNIT	PAPER NUMBER
2540	3

DATE MAILED: 1998 Oct 9

This is a communication from the examiner in charge of your application.

COMMISSIONER OF PATENTS AND TRADEMARKS

Response Due 1999 Jan 9 P.B.

☑ This application has been examined   ☐ Responsive to communication filed on _____   ☐ This action is made final.

A shortened statutory period for response to this action is set to expire **3** month(s), **0** days from the date of this letter.
Failure to respond within the period for response will cause the application to become abandoned.   35 U.S.C. 133

Part I   THE FOLLOWING ATTACHMENT(S) ARE PART OF THIS ACTION:

1. ☑ Notice of References Cited by Examiner, PTO-892.
2. ☑ Notice re Patent Drawing, PTO-948.
3. ☐ Notice of Art Cited by Applicant, PTO-1449.
4. ☐ Notice of Informal Patent Application, Form PTO-152
5. ☐ Information on How to Effect Drawing Changes, PTO-1474.
6. ☐ _____

Part II   SUMMARY OF ACTION

1. ☑ Claims **1-7** are pending in the application.

   Of the above, claims _____ are withdrawn from consideration.

2. ☐ Claims _____ have been cancelled.

3. ☐ Claims _____ are allowed.

4. ☑ Claims **1-7** are rejected.

5. ☐ Claims _____ are objected to.

6. ☐ Claims _____ are subject to restriction or election requirement.

7. ☑ This application has been filed with informal drawings which are acceptable for examination purposes until such time as allowable subject matter is indicated.

8. ☐ Allowable subject matter having been indicated, formal drawings are required in response to this Office action.

9. ☐ The corrected or substitute drawings have been received on _____. These drawings are ☐ acceptable; ☐ not acceptable (see explanation).

10. ☐ The ☐ proposed drawing correction and/or the ☐ proposed additional or substitute sheet(s) of drawings, filed on _____ has (have) been ☐ approved by the examiner. ☐ disapproved by the examiner (see explanation).

11. ☐ The proposed drawing correction, filed _____, has been ☐ approved. ☐ disapproved (see explanation). However, the Patent and Trademark Office no longer makes drawing changes. It is now applicant's responsibility to ensure that the drawings are corrected. Corrections MUST be effected in accordance with the instructions set forth on the attached letter "INFORMATION ON HOW TO EFFECT DRAWING CHANGES", PTO-1474.

12. ☐ Acknowledgment is made of the claim for priority under 35 U.S.C. 119. The certified copy has ☐ been received ☐ not been received ☐ been filed in parent application, serial no. _____; filed on _____.

13. ☐ Since this application appears to be in condition for allowance except for formal matters, prosecution as to the merits is closed in accordance with the practice under Ex parte Quayle, 1935 C.D. 11; 453 O.G. 213.

14. ☐ Other

PTOL-326 (Rev. 7-82)   EXAMINER'S ACTION

Figure 6A—Sample Office Action

Serial No. 07/345,678

-2-

Art Unit 254

The drawing is objected to under Rule 1.83(a) in that all the features recited in the claims are not shown. See Claims 1 and 2 regarding the "electronic counter means" and "first and second solid state counters."

The specification is objected to under Rule 1.71(b) as inadequate. In particular, there is insufficient information regarding the "counter," "counter memory" and how the counter controls the illumination of the lights. Applicant is required to amplify the disclosure in this regard without the introduction of new matter, 608.04 MPEP.

Claims 1-7 are rejected under 35 U.S.C. § 112, 1st. paragraph, as based on an insufficient disclosure. See above.

Insofar as adequate, Claims 1-6 are rejected under 35 U.S.C. § 102(b) as fully anticipated by Ohman. Ohman shows an electronic cribbage board counter that fully meets these claims. See Fig. 1. The microprocessor 300 shown in Fig. 3 inherently includes the counter means of Claims 1 and 2.

Claim 7 is rejected under 35 U.S.C. § 112, ¶ 2. The term "said LCD readout" lacks proper antecedent basis in parent independent claim 1 as claim 1 recites only an "LCD monitor."

Figure 6A—Sample Office Action (continued)

Claim 7 is rejected under 35 U.S.C. § 103 as unpatentable over Ohman in view of Morin. Ohman shows an electronic cribbage board counter, as stated. Morin shows an LCD tally monitor. It would be obvious to substitute Morin's LCD tally monitor for Ohman's mechanical readout, since the substitution of LCD readouts for mechanical readouts is an expedient well known to those skilled in the art. See column 13, lines 34-41 of Morin, which indicate that in lieu of the LCD readout shown, other types of readouts may be used.

No claim is allowed.

The remaining art cited shows other electronic board games containing the claimed structure. Note Morin, which shows the details of a computer as containing first and second counter means.

Any inquiry concerning this communication should be directed to Examiner Heyman at telephone number 703-557-4777.

Heyman/EW

98/10/9

John S. Heyman

Examiner

Group Art Unit 254

Figure 6A—Sample Office Action (continued)

4. Claims 1 to 6 are rejected because the examiner does not believe they are novel when compared to another invention (as identified in the "Ohman" patent). This rejection is based on Section 102 of the patent laws (35 U.S.C. § 102).

5. Claim 7 is rejected because there is no identical antecedent (or direct reference) in Claim 1. The applicant has failed to follow a technical drafting rule. This objection is based on Section 112 of the patent laws (35 U.S.C. § 112).

6. Claim 7 is rejected a second time as being obvious. The examiner believes that based on two prior references, this claim would have been obvious to someone skilled in the field of the invention. This rejection is based on Section 103 of the patent laws (35 U.S.C. § 103).

If the examiner cites any prior-art references in the office action, those references will be listed on an attached page.

3. Amendment in Response to First Office Action

The first office action will specify the time period (usually three months) by which a response (known as an "amendment") must be filed. The response usually includes some or all of the following:

- a summary of the amendments

- a review of the rejections made by the examiner
- a review of the references cited by the examiner
- a summary of how the applicant changed the claims
- a statement of distinctions and arguments as to prior-art references
- a request for reconsideration of the examiner's position
- a discussion of dependent and other main claims
- a discussion of any technical (Section 112) rejections
- a request that the examiner write the claims, and
- a conclusion.

Most rejections of claims are based upon prior art and are categorized either as Section 102 rejections (the invention is not novel) or Section 103 rejections (the invention is novel but obvious). If the rejection is based on Section 103, the examiner is tacitly admitting that the claims are novel.

If a prior-art reference is strikingly similar to the claim, the claim is said to "read on" the prior art. In these cases, the claim must be amended, usually by narrowing it.

If it can be proven that the date of invention is earlier than the effective date of the reference, the applicant can "swear behind" and eliminate the reference (PTO Rule 131). The date of invention is the earliest of (1) the filing date of the regular application or PPA, (2) the date of building and testing, or (3) the date of conception followed by diligence (see Chapter 2, Section D). The effective date of any U.S. patent reference is its filing date; the effective date of any other reference is its publication date. MPEP § 715 and PTO Rules provide more details as well as limitations on the applicant's right to "swear behind."

The Applicant's Duty to Disclose

If you are the applicant, you have a duty to disclose all information known to you, such as relevant prior art, which bears on the patentability of the invention (see Chapter 2, Section D). If a prior-art reference is found that is so similar that it makes your invention unpatentable, your application should be abandoned. As a general rule, you do not have to (and shouldn't) admit or state anything negative about your invention.

Nothing New Added

An applicant can never add new matter to an application (PTO Rule 118). New matter is any technical information, including dimensions, materials, etc., that was not present in the application as originally filed.

Fax Now Available, Email Is Coming. Amendments, petitions, appeals, and elections (but not applications, fees or drawings) can be filed by fax. Faxed papers must include a statement, *"I certify I have transmitted this paper by fax to the Patent and Trademark Office at* [time] *on* [date].*"* The PTO will consider the paper as having been filed on the date of transmission, or the next business day if the applicant faxes it on a non-business day. The PTO has provided email addresses and Internet access for many of its employees. Email communications may be used for minor matters, such as status requests, minor corrections in a paper, notification that a communication has been sent, and more, but not major papers, such as amendments and patent applications. The email address for PTO employees is provided on office actions. Since email is not a secure form of communication and the PTO is obligated to preserve all patent applications in secret, PTO employees are not allowed to send email containing any sensitive information unless specifically authorized by the applicant.

The following statement must be included in the application: *"Recognizing that Internet communications are not secure, I hereby authorize the PTO to communicate with me concerning any subject matter of this application by electronic mail. I understand that a copy of these communications will be made of record in the application file."*

4. Second and Final Office Action

A second office action, usually designated a "final" office action, is mailed within two to six months of filing the first amendment. This is supposed to end the prosecution stage, but as explained in Section B, a "final action" is rarely final.

When the Second Office Action Isn't Final

In some cases, the examiner's second office action may not be final, for example if the examiner cites new references that were not necessitated by the applicant's amendments. In that case, the applicant responds as if it were a first office action (see Section A2).

---

5. Notice of Allowance, Issue Fee, and Official Patent Deed

If the amendment is sufficient and the examiner is convinced that the application meets the requirements of patentability, a Notice of Allowance is sent and an issue fee is due within three months. A "Notice of Allowability" is usually mailed with the Notice of Allowance. This document merely states that the claims are all allowed and a Notice of Allowance is attached indicating whether formal drawings are due.

Several months after the fee is paid and formal drawings are filed, an Issue Notifica-

tion is sent from the PTO indicating the issue date and number of the patent. On the Tuesday that the patent issues, the PTO mails the official "Letters Patent" deed.

6. Reviving the Dead: Recovering From Technical Abandonment

A reply to an office action requiring substantive changes must be made within three months from the mailing date of the office action. A reply to an office action requiring non-substantive changes must be made within one month. If these deadlines are not met, the application is technically abandoned, meaning that it cannot be pursued further at the PTO. However, the application can usually be "revived" or extended in any of the three following ways:

- **Buying an Extension (PTO Rules 136(a) and 17(a)-(d)).** If a reply is not made within the designated period, it can still be made at any time up to the sixth month from the office action mailing date by buying an extension from the PTO. The extension cannot be purchased to extend any response period beyond six months and also can't extend the three-month statutory period from the Notice of Allowance.
- **Petition to Revive If Delay Was "Unavoidable" (PTO Rules 137(a) or 316(b), and 17(c)).** A petition can be filed to revive the application within six months of the date of abandonment if the delay was "unavoidable," for

example, the office action was never received or the applicant suffered a severe illness.

- **Petition to Revive If Delay Was Avoidable but Unintentional (PTO Rules 137(b) or 316(c), and 17(m)).** A petition can be filed to revive the application within the three-month period if the delay was "avoidable but unintentional," for example, the applicant misinterpreted the time to reply to the office action. A higher fee is charged than if the delay was unavoidable.

B. Responding to a Final Office Action

A "final" action doesn't mean that PTO prosecution has ended; it means that the examiner is cutting off the applicant's right to change the claims in the application. The applicant has the following options:

1. Convincing the Examiner

An applicant can ask the examiner to reconsider a final office action. This can be done in writing, by phone, or in person. Another amendment, known as an "after-final amendment," can also be filed. If the examiner is not convinced, an "advisory action" will be sent reiterating the examiner's position. The applicant still has the opportunity to exercise the other choices in this section.

2. Complying With the Examiner's Request

The claims can be amended as suggested by the examiner.

3. Filing a Continuation, Continuation-in-Part or a Request for Continued Examination

An inventor can have claims reviewed further by the examiner by filing a continuation application or a request for continued examination (RCE).

A new application, known as a "continuation," can be filed while the original (or "parent") application is still pending. A continuation application consists of the same invention, cross-referenced to the parent application and with a new set of claims. The continuation application allows a second or third bite at the apple since it's theoretically possible to file an unlimited sequence of continuation applications. The filing date of the parent application is retained for purposes of determining the relevancy of prior art.

> **EXAMPLE:** Jim filed a patent application for his paint roller invention in January 2000. He filed a continuation application for the paint roller in July 2002. Bob invented the same paint roller device in January 2001. Jim has priority because his parent application was filed before Bob invented his paint roller.

If a Request for Continued Examination is filed, the inventor does not have to file a new copy of the specification or drawing and will not receive a new serial number or filing date. The inventor files an REC form, pays another filing fee, and submits another amendment.

A less common form of extension application is known as a continuation-in-part (CIP) in which a portion or all of the earlier application is continued and new matter not disclosed in the earlier application is included. CIP applications are used when an applicant wants to present an improvement but is prevented from adding it to a pending application because of the prohibition against adding "new matter" (see sidebar above—Nothing New Added).

EXAMPLE: Luther invents a bicycle gear with a new shape. After Luther files the patent application, his research shows that the gear works much more quietly if it's made of a certain alloy. Luther wants to add a few dependent claims specifically to cover a gear made of the alloy. The solution: file a CIP describing the alloy in the specification and add a few dependent claims that recite that the gear is made of the alloy. To avoid any possibility of double patenting, Luther abandons the parent application or files a terminal disclaimer, a statement that both patents will terminate on the date when the first patent ends (see Section C5).

When a CIP is filed, the parent application is usually allowed to go abandoned because if the claims in the CIP and parent application are similar, one or both of the resulting patents can be held invalid under a principle known as double patenting (see Section C5). If the claims are different, both applications can proceed. For further information on continuations, review MPEP § 201.07.

Continuations and the 20 Year Term. If a continuation application is filed, the resulting patent will expire 20 years after the filing date of the original, or parent, application.

4. Appeal

An applicant who believes that the examiner's final office action is wrong can appeal to the Board of Appeals and Patent Interferences (BAPI), a tribunal of PTO judges. In addition to filing written arguments, an oral hearing can be requested during which oral statements can be provided for 20 minutes. For further information on complying with the appeal procedure, see PTO Rules of Practice 191 to 198.

After the appeal brief is filed, the examiner re-examines the application and files a response, usually maintaining the rejection (the "Examiner's Answer"). An applicant can file a response to the Examiner's Answer. The Board either agrees with the applicant and instructs the examiner to allow the application or the appeal is rejected (which happens in two-thirds of appeals) and the Final Office Action stands. The applicant can file a further appeal to the Court of Appeals for the Federal Circuit (CAFC) within 60 days of the decision. If the CAFC upholds the PTO's decision, the applicant can request the United States Supreme Court hear the case, although the Supreme Court rarely hears patent appeals. If a patent is finally issued as a result of an appeal, the PTO will extend the patent term up to five years based on the delay. (35 U.S.C. § 154.)

Petitions to the Commissioner for Non-Substantive Matters

In cases where unfair or illegal treatment is alleged, the Commissioner of Patents and Trademarks has the power to overrule almost anyone in the PTO except the BAPI. For example, if someone in the PTO's application branch decides that an application is not entitled to a certain filing date, the applicant can petition the Commissioner to overrule this decision. If the final office action is premised on unfair or illegal treatment, a petition that includes a verified statement signed by the applicant must be filed promptly. Verified statements are either notarized or contain a declaration attesting to the truthfulness of the statement.

5. Abandonment

If a response to the final office action is not filed within the three-month period, the PTO mails a Notice of Abandonment and the application process is officially over.

 Keeping Others From Pursuing Your Abandoned Application. Some applicants decide to abandon an application but also want to prevent anyone else from getting a valid patent on the same invention. This can be accomplished by converting the application to a Statutory Invention Registration (SIR). The SIR precludes anyone else from obtaining a patent on the invention with the exception of someone who filed before the applicant. As a practical matter, the same result can be achieved at a lesser cost by filing with businesses known as invention register companies, such as ITD, Technotec, or *Research Disclosure* Magazine.

C. Additional Application Issues

In this section we discuss interferences, divisional applications, reissue applications, substitute applications, and double patenting. All of these topics relate to problems that may arise during patent prosecution.

1. Interferences

An interference is a costly, complex PTO proceeding to determine who will get a patent when two or more applicants are claiming the same invention. In other words, it is a method of sorting out inventorship priority. Approximately 2% of applications become involved in interferences. The PTO institutes an interference when two patent applications are filed claiming the same invention. Occasionally, an interference may involve a patent that has been in force for less than one year. During an interference, the PTO determines which inventor first reduced the invention to practice. (For more information regarding reduction to practice, see Chapter 3, Section E.)

2. Divisional Applications

If a patent application contains more than one invention, the PTO will require that it be "restricted" to just one of the inventions. That's because the application fee entitles an applicant to have only one invention examined. Generally speaking, it's very difficult to successfully argue against (or "traverse") this type of PTO-imposed restriction. The only solution to protect several inventions claimed in the original application is to file a divisional application. The official definition of a divisional application is "a later application for a distinct or indepen-

dent invention, carved out of a pending application and disclosing and claiming only subject matter disclosed in the earlier or parent application" (MPEP 201.06). A divisional application is entitled to the filing date of the parent case for purposes of overcoming prior art. The divisional application must be filed while the parent application is pending.

When the Public Protests Against Allowance. If a member of the public, such as another inventor, is aware of information that is adverse to a pending application, this information may be brought to the attention of the examiner in the form of a protest by sending the information to the PTO and identifying the application as specifically as possible.

NASA Declarations

If an application relates to aerospace, the PTO will send a form letter (PTOL-224) with the filing receipt or after the application is allowed. The letter will state that because the invention relates to aerospace, a declaration is required stating the "full facts" regarding the making of the applicant's invention. This is to guarantee that NASA has no rights in it. A Notice of Allowance will not be issued if the declaration isn't filed.

3. Reissue Applications

A reissue application is an attempt to correct information in an issued patent. It is usually filed when a patent owner believes:

- the claims are not broad enough
- the claims are too broad (the applicant discovered a new reference), or
- there are significant errors in the specification.

In these cases, an attempt is made to correct the patent by filing an application to have the original patent reissued at any time during its term. The reissue patent will take the place of the original patent and expire at the same time as the original patent would have expired. If the purpose is to broaden the claims of the patent through a reissue application, the applicant must do so within two years from the date the original patent issued. There is a risk in filing a reissue application because all of the claims of the original patent will be examined and can be rejected.

4. Substitute Applications

If a patent application is abandoned, a substitute application can be filed that is essentially a duplicate of the abandoned application (see MPEP 201.09). The disadvantage of a substitute application is that the filing date of the previously abandoned patent application is not retained. Any prior art occurring after the filing date of the

earlier case can be used against the substitute case. If the substitute application issues into a patent, the patent will expire 20 years from the filing date of the substitute.

5. Double Patenting

If a patent is issued and the patent owner files a second application containing the same invention ("double patenting"), the second application will be rejected, or if the second application resulted in a patent, that patent will be invalidated. What does it mean when two applications contain the same invention? It means either that the two inventions are literally the same or that the second invention is an obvious modification of the first invention.

EXAMPLE: An inventor applied for a patent on polymer dispersants used in motor oil to keep engines clean. A patent issued in 1989. A continuation application was filed incorporating similar, but slightly broader claims. The Court of Appeals for the Federal Circuit (see Section B4) ruled that the continuation application was invalid for double patenting because it was an obvious modification of the first application. (*In re Emert*, 124 F.3d 1458 (CAFC 1997).)

In the example above, the applicant could avoid double patenting by agreeing that both patents would terminate on the date when the first patent ended (known as a "terminal disclaimer").

D. Design Patent Prosecution

Design patent prosecution is much simpler than regular patent prosecution and rarely requires more than elementary changes. Usually, the examiner tells the applicant exactly what to do.

The drawings are the key element since the claims in a design patent are presented visually, not by words. To be patentable, the appearance of the applicant's design, as a whole, must be nonobvious to a designer of ordinary skill over the references (usually earlier design patents) cited by the examiner. Since many companies may modify their patented designs, multiple design patent applications are often filed to separately claim the various ways that the design may be embodied.

It takes at least a year to get a design patent and the design patent is effective for 14 years. There are no maintenance fees. An applicant can convert a design application to a utility application, or vice versa, by filing a continuing application under 35 U.S.C. 120. However, this is rarely done as it is very difficult to convert a design application to a utility application without adding new matter (see sidebar above—Nothing New Added). ■

Chapter 7

Patent Ownership

atent ownership can be a contentious issue. After all, the owner is the person entitled to control the manufacture and sale of the inventions covered in the patent. For some patents this can mean the beginning of a dynasty that lasts long after the patent expires. If Clarence Birdseye had not owned a patent for packaging frozen foods, it is unlikely the Birdseye company would be here today. The same might be true for John Mason who owned the patent for Mason jars.

This chapter is about the issues that arise when inventors, employers, or co-inventors assert ownership rights. In Section A, we discuss the single inventor's situation. In Section B, we discuss the situation where an inventor gives up complete or partial ownership to an employer, usually under an employment agreement. In Section C, we address the complications of joint patent ownership, for example, when more than one person creates a patentable invention.

A. The Inventor Is Initial Owner of Patent Rights

An inventor is an "idea" person who creates the novelty of the invention. An inventor has the inventive concepts that make the invention different and nonobvious and become the basis for the patent claims. The claims are the "heart" of the patent application and are described in Chapter 5,

Section C. Often, the inventor retains ownership and exploits the patent by licensing or selling rights to others or manufactures and sells the invention and enjoys monopoly rights. A license is permission for others to make use or sell the invention for a limited period of time in exchange for royalty payments.

In other cases, the inventor is not prepared or able to market or license the invention and permanently transfers patent rights under an assignment. An assignment is a complete or partial transfer of patent ownership. Assignments are almost always made in return for payment, although in rare cases, an inventor may assign patent rights in order to benefit humanity. For example, Dr. Frederick Banting had no interest in the money from his pioneering process of controlling diabetes through insulin injections and assigned his patent rights to the University of Toronto.

B. Employee Inventions

Generally, most employed inventors are obligated to transfer rights in their inventions to their employer. This occurs in one of three ways:

- An employment agreement includes provisions that require the employee to give up all rights in advance of creating an invention. Because these employment agreements are signed before the employee creates the invention, they are sometimes referred to as pre-invention assignments

- The employee was hired specifically for the purposes of creating an invention (a principle known as "employed to invent," or "hired to invent," see Section B).
- The employer acquires limited patent rights under a principle known as a "shop right" (see Section B3).

The subject of employee inventions is covered in more detail in *License Your Invention*, by Richard Stim (Nolo).

1. Employment Agreements

The majority of businesses that employ inventors, designers, and engineers require that each employee sign an employment agreement that establishes the circumstances under which the business owns employee-created inventions.

For example, in 1974, a scientist for the Minnesota Mining and Manufacturing Company (3M) was singing in a church choir when he realized that an adhesive substance produced at 3M could be affixed to paper and used to mark sections in his hymnal without damaging the book. The result was Post-It notes, one of the most successful office products in history. Although the scientist conceived of the idea on his own time, he had signed an employment agreement with 3M that

contained a pre-invention assignment provision. Therefore 3M acquired all rights in the invention.

Most pre-invention assignments require that the employee-inventor assign all inventions to the employers that are:

- made during the term of employment
- related to the employer's existing or contemplated business
- made by using the employer's time (that is, the time for which the employee is paid), facilities, or materials, or
- made as a result of activity within the scope of the employee's duties.

If an employment agreement contains a pre-invention assignment provision such as this, the employee will not own inventions that fall under the agreement. If the employee disregards the agreement and attempts to patent and license an invention, the employer will be able to sue for breach of the employment agreement and if the employer wins the lawsuit, the employee may have to pay monetary damages and transfer ownership of the patent to the employer.

It is important to note that under many employment agreements, even if an employee makes an invention at home, on the employee's own time, the employer can still be entitled to ownership. Equally important, the employed inventor is usually bound to disclose all inventions to the employer (so the employer can determine if they're assignable).

Disclosing an invention simply means that the employee-inventor must report the invention; it does not necessarily mean that the inventor must give up rights. The final determination depends on the terms of the employment agreement and the law of the state in which the employee inventor works (see sidebar, below, Limitations on Pre-Invention Assignments).

If, after disclosure, the employer isn't interested in the invention, the employee can apply for a release. This is a document under which the employer reassigns or returns the invention to the employee. The employer may retain a "shop right" under the release. A shop right is a nontransferable right to use the invention for its own purposes and business only. This shop right is discussed in Section B3.

Employment agreements also usually require the employee to keep good records of inventions made and to cooperate in signing patent applications and giving testimony when needed, even after termination of employment. In addition, these agreements often contain a "power of attorney" provision that guarantees the employer can register and administer the ownership rights without the employee, even if the employee is willing and able to assist.

Who Is Listed in the Patent Application

In the U.S., the true inventor must always be named as the applicant in a patent application even if the inventor has made a pre-invention assignment. However, the employee will be required to sign an assignment (a legal transfer) of patent rights to the employer. This assignment is also filed with the PTO. Under the assignment, the employer acquires all patent rights and is listed in the patent as the assignee (owner) although the employee will be listed as the applicant inventor.

Some companies give the employee a cash bonus when the employee signs a company patent application. This bonus is not payment for signing (the employee's wages are supposed to cover that) but to encourage employees to invent and turn in invention disclosures on their inventions. Some employers, such as Lockheed, give their inventor-employees a generous cut of the royalties from their invention. Some will even set up a subsidiary entity (partly owned by the employee-inventor) to exploit the invention. Most, however, prefer to reward highly creative employees via the salary route.

Legislation has been proposed to expand the rights of the employed inventor. Various engineering organizations have also proposed methods of expanding employee rights. One of these proposals is to convert to a system where employees own their inventions but usually assign them to their employers in return for a generous cut (such as 20%) of the profits or royalties.

Limitations on Pre-Invention Assignments

Five states (California, Illinois, Minnesota, North Carolina, and Washington) have laws that limit pre-invention assignments. Regardless of what is stated in the employment agreement, an employer cannot claim ownership of an invention if it:

- is created with the employer's resources
- does not result from work performed for an employer, and
- does not relate to the employer's business.

These laws can be found in the following state codes: Cal. Lab. Code §§ 2870-2872, Ill. Rev. Stat. ch. 140, para. 302; Minn. Stat. § 181.78; N.C. Gen. Stat. §§ 66-57.1, .2; Wash. Rev. Code Ann. §§ 49.44.140, .150.

2. Employed to Invent

It is possible that even without a written employment agreement, an employer may own rights to an employee-created invention under the "employed to invent" doctrine. How does this rule apply? If an inventor is employed—even without a written employment agreement—to accomplish a defined task, or is hired or directed to create an invention, the employer will own all rights to the subsequent invention. This doctrine is derived from a Supreme Court ruling that stated, "One employed to make an invention, who succeeds, during his term of service, in accomplishing that task, is bound to assign to his employer any patent obtained." (*Standard Parts Co. v. Peck*, 264 U.S. 52 (1924).)

Generally, most companies prefer to use a written agreement because it is more reliable and easier to enforce than this implied agreement. However, the issue of "employed to invent" still arises. For example in one case, an engineer had no written employment agreement with his employer and was assigned as the chief engineer on a project to devise a process of welding a "leading edge" for turbine engines. Even though there was no pre-invention assignment, a court held that the company owned the patent rights because the engineer was hired for the express purpose of creating the process.

3. Shop Rights

The previous two situations (written employment agreements and the "employed to invent" rule) allow the employer to become the owner of all patent rights. There is another situation in which the employer may not acquire ownership of the patent or trade secret, but may acquire a limited right, known as a "shop right," to use these innovations. Under a shop right, the employee retains ownership of the patent, but the employer has a right to use the invention without paying the inventor.

A shop right can occur only if the inventor uses the employer's resources (materials, supplies, time) to create an invention. Other circumstances may be relevant, but use of employer resources is the most important criteria. Shop right principles are derived from state laws and precedents in court cases. Generally, the shop right claim arises when an inventor sues a former employer for patent infringement. The employer defends itself by claiming a shop right.

For example, in 1982, a consultant for a power company was hired to install and maintain an electrostatic precipitator. However, the power company was not happy with the operation of the device. The consultant, observing the problems, conceived of an innovation that would detect particles of ash. The power company installed the device at several locations and the consultant, who later acquired a patent, sued for infringement. A federal court ruled that the power company had a shop right since the consultant had developed the invention while working at the power company and using the power company's resources. This shop right situation is distinguished from the "employed to invent" scenario described in Section B2, because in the shop right case, the consultant's invention was not the subject of the consulting contract—he was not hired to invent. However, since he used the power company's resources to create the invention, the company acquired a shop right.

An inventor should be concerned about shop rights only if the invention is created on the employer's time or using the employer's resources (materials, supplies, or trade secrets). If it isn't, the shop right rule is irrelevant.

4. University Employee Inventions

Most colleges and universities require that faculty execute formal agreements which grant the university rights to all discoveries made by employees using its labs, equipment, or other resources. Normally, when an invention or discovery is successful and results in a licensing deal, the school pays some portion of the revenues to the inventor. At one major university, for example, inventors get 50% of the first $100,000 of net revenue, 40% of the second $100,000 and 30% of any sums after that. But if there's no ownership agreement, the deal might be quite different, as demonstrated in the example below.

EXAMPLE: In the mid-sixties, Robert Cade, a professor of medicine at the University of Florida, created a high-energy drink that provided electrolyte replacement for perspiring athletes. The potion eventually came to be sold under the trademark, *Gatorade*. At the time, the University of Florida and Dr. Cade had no written agreement regarding the ownership of employee-created inventions. On his own, Cade licensed Gatorade to a food company and started reaping huge revenues. The university felt it should own the rights to the drink and sued. Also, the government got into the suit because it provided grants for Cade's research. After a long three-party lawsuit, the parties settled and the university was reportedly awarded 20% of the professor's share. The university's share is estimated to be over $4 million a year from the licensing of the Gatorade formula. The Gatorade drink generates over $1 billion in annual sales.

 Inventions Prepared Under Government Contracts. According to a federal policy implemented in 1983, federal agencies may waive or omit patent rights when awarding government contracts (although there are some exceptions for space research, nuclear energy, and defense). If an inventor contracts directly with the federal government—and is not working for the federal government through a private company—the inventor should ask about patent ownership at the time of contracting.

C. Joint Owners

When more than one person creates a patentable invention, the joint inventors share credit in the patent application and share in the patent ownership as joint patent owners. However, to acquire joint-inventor status, each person must contribute an inventive concept that becomes part of at least one patent claim. Unfortunately, issues

about joint ownership often lead to contentious disputes between inventors. For example, the diabetes researcher, Dr. Banting, mentioned in Section A, was so angered by an associate taking credit for his insulin research, that he tackled him at the university, knocking his head against the floor. As indicated in the following sections, most joint owner disputes are less violent and more concerned with the issue of compensation. The primary issue is often whether an associate is entitled to co-inventor status.

1. Establishing and Proving Joint Invention

As proving co-inventor status can sometimes be difficult, the best way to avoid problems is for all inventors to keep a lab notebook. A lab notebook is a technical diary which faithfully records all developments and is frequently signed by the inventor(s) and witnesses. In Chapter 3, we discuss recordkeeping and inventor notebooks. In addition, many disputes can be avoided by the use of a Consultant's Agreement in which persons working with an inventor agree to assign all rights in their work to the inventor. Absent such documentation, or agreement, expensive disputes can arise, with only vague memories to deal with.

Joint inventors need not have worked together either physically or at the same time, and each need not have made the same type or amount of contribution. To qualify as a joint inventor, as stated, an inventor need merely have contributed something to at least one claim of the application.

Determining whether a contribution is substantial can sometimes be difficult. For instance, if one person came up with the concept of the invention, while the other merely built and tested it—the second person is not a co-inventor. It is not enough to build and test an invention. The joint inventor must make a contribution to at least one novel and nonobvious concept that makes the invention patentable.

On the other hand, if one person came up with the idea for an invention and the model maker then came up with valuable suggestions and contributions that went beyond the skill of an ordinary model maker and made the invention work far better, both people should be named as co-inventors on the patent application, provided the model maker's contribution is present in at least one claim.

EXAMPLE: Dr. Wilcox developed a device that could be attached to a computer modem and could triple its output. However, Dr. Wilcox was stumped as to how to increase the input. Sarah, an engineering student constructing his device, suggested a novel compression method that allowed Dr. Wilcox to triple the input telephone transfer rate. Sarah's contribution found its way into the claims of a patent ap-

plication. Dr. Wilcox and Sarah are joint-inventors.

2. When a Patent Application Fails to List Joint Inventors

If an error is made in listing the inventors on a patent application, and the mistake was made with deceptive intent, it can affect the ability to enforce the patent and may result in loss of patent rights. For example, if a biotech company, in bad faith, fails to name two additional inventors in its chromatography patent, a court can prevent the company from enforcing patent rights against a competitor.

If the error in the patent was not made in bad faith, the mistake can be corrected without any loss of rights under PTO Rule 48 (patent applications) or PTO Rule 324 (patents). (See Chapter 6 for more information on correcting patents.)

3. Patent Laws and the Effect of Joint Ownership

Usually, the joint owners decide amongst themselves how to split the revenue from sales and licensing under the terms of a joint owner agreement (see Section C4). If the joint owners cannot decide and a dispute results, a court will make the final determination. However, there are some special rules regarding joint ownership and division of income from patents. First, all joint owners must consent to an assignment of all rights to the patent. In other words, no joint owner can give up *all* rights to the invention. However, unless prohibited by an agreement with the other owners, any joint owner can make, sell, or use the invention without the consent of the other owners and without compensating the other owners. This is the result of a patent law that states, "In the absence of any agreement to the contrary, each of the joint owners of a patent may make, use, offer to sell, or sell the patented invention within the United States, or import the patented invention into the United States, without the consent of and without accounting to the other owners." (Title 35 of the United States Code, § 262.)

This statute may prevent a joint owner from being rewarded for any inventive contribution. In the case of an investor who has purchased a patent interest, the statute can prevent the investor from being rewarded for making a capital contribution. The statute also works a severe hardship if one joint owner works hard to engineer and develop a market for the patented product and another joint owner steps in as a competitor. Seem unfair? The only way for the joint owners of a patented invention to protect their interest is to enter into a Joint Ownership Agreement, as provided below.

4. Joint Ownership Agreements

Problems commonly arise in situations where there are joint owners. These include questions as to who is entitled to commercially exploit the invention, who owns the financial shares, and what type of accounting must be performed on partnership books. In addition the inequitable results of 35 U.S.C. § 262, (as described in Section C3) may deprive a patent owner of reward for invention or investment. Fortunately, most of these problems can be minimized or eliminated by the use of a Joint Owners' Agreement (JOA).

A typical JOA:

- prohibits any joint owner from exploiting the patent without the other joint owners' consent, except that if there is a dissenter, a majority can act if consultation is unsuccessful
- provides a method of resolving disputes, for example, in case of an equally divided vote, the parties will select an arbiter, whose decision shall break the tie
- provides that the joint owners shall share profits proportionally, according to their interests in expenditures and income. In the event that one owner does not agree to an expenditure, the others can advance the amount in question, subject to an increased reimbursement (often double the expenditure) from any income
- provides that if an owner desires to manufacture or sell the patented invention, that owner must pay a reasonable royalty to all other owners, including the manufacturing owner.

Copies of joint ownership agreements can be found in *Patent It Yourself*, by attorney David Pressman (Nolo) and in *License Your Invention*, by attorney Richard Stim (Nolo).

5. Methods of Acquiring Joint Ownership

In the previous sections we described how joint invention leads to joint ownership. However there are methods of acquiring a joint ownership interest other than by invention. Below we highlight some examples:

Joint Ownership Created by Assignment for Money. In return for a payment or for other investment in the invention process, an inventor may convey a portion of a patent to an investor.

> EXAMPLE: Tom invents a metal detector that works underwater. He needs money to build a prototype and to promote the invention. Jerry agrees to give Tom $100,000 in return for an assignment of 50% ownership interest in the invention. Tom and Jerry become joint owners. However, Jerry would not be listed in the patent application as an inventor, only as the assignee of a partial interest in the invention.

Joint Ownership Created by Will. Upon the death of a patent owner, the patent rights, like any property right, can be passed to two or more heirs or beneficiaries.

> EXAMPLE: Sam patents a process for scrambling and cooking eggs within their shells. He dies and in his will he leaves half ownership interest in the invention to his daughter Carol, and the other half to Dartmouth College. Carol and Dartmouth become joint owners.

Joint Ownership Created by Assignment to a Partnership. If a patent owner transfers a patent to a partnership, each partner becomes a joint patent owner.

> EXAMPLE: Jill invents a new style of camping stove. Ian wants to invest money to perfect the invention. Jim, a lawyer, wants to contribute his legal and licensing experience to help license the invention. Jill, Ian, and Jim form a partnership and Jill assigns the invention to the partnership. Each partner is a joint owner in the invention. ■

Chapter 8

Patent Infringement

Patent infringement is the unauthorized act of making, using, selling, offering for sale, or importing a patented invention. Allowing patent infringement to occur can have disastrous results for a patent owner as revenues from a patented invention are siphoned away by a competitor. On the other hand, the results may even be more disastrous if the owner sues the competitor and the patent is successfully challenged. For example, Hoffman-LaRoche, an international drug company, sued a smaller company, Promega, over the use of a patent for a process for analyzing DNA. Promega successfully defended itself by arguing that the DNA patent was invalid because the inventors had misled patent examiners. The ruling allows anyone to use, sell, or make the patented invention freely even though Hoffman-La Roche paid $300 million for the patent. As you can see, enforcing patent rights can be tricky, expensive, and sometimes risky. In this chapter, we discuss the ways that a patent can be infringed and the procedures for dealing with infringement.

A. What Is Patent Infringement?

Infringement occurs when someone makes, uses, sells, offers for sale, or imports a patented invention without permission from the patent owner. These types of acts are referred to as "direct infringement."

To make an infringing invention means to construct or manufacture the parts of the patented device without permission from the owner. For example, a patent on an electronic key ring is infringed when a factory manufactures the key rings without permission.

To use an infringing invention means to practice (or use) an invention without the permission from the patent owner. For example, a patent on a process for making an integrated circuit chip is infringed every time the process is used to make a chip.

To sell an infringing invention means to sell a patented invention without permission from the patent owner. It is also illegal to offer to sell an infringing invention. An offer to sell can include solicitations and advertisements, for example, if a company emails a proposal to sell an infringing device.

To import an infringing invention means to bring a patented invention into the United States without permission from the patent owner. For example, a company infringes when it imports a patented automobile spark plug into the U.S. without the U.S. patent owner's authorization.

It can also be an infringement to contribute to or persuade someone else to do one of the acts described above. This is referred to as "indirect infringement." For example, it is contributory infringement to convince someone to import infringing merchandise.

Defendants and Plaintiffs

The terms "plaintiff' and "defendant" are used throughout this chapter. The plaintiff is usually the patent owner who believes that a patent has been infringed and initiates a lawsuit. The defendant is the party accused of infringement.

1. Only Patent Claims Can Be Infringed

To infringe a patent, the infringing device must physically have or perform all of the elements contained in one of the patent claims. (See Chapter 5, Section C, to learn more about patent claims.) A device containing additional elements will also infringe. For example, if a patent claim recites three elements, A, B, and C, and the infringing device has four elements, A, B, C, and D, it will infringe. But if the infringing device has only two of the three elements, A and B, it won't infringe.

2. Patent Owner's Permission

An essential element of infringement is that it occurs without the patent owner's authorization. When a patent owner has authorized a use, anything that exceeds that authorization is also an infringement. For example, a company that was authorized to build and use one machine built two machines, although it only used one at a time. The building of the second machine was an infringement.

3. When a Patent Can Be Infringed

A patent can be infringed only "during the term of the patent." This means that the patent must be issued in order for the patent owner to sue for infringement. A patent owner cannot sue for infringement during the "pendency period," that is the time between filing of the patent application and issuance of the patent.

However, under the new 18-month publication statute, an inventor whose application is published prior to issuance may obtain royalties from an infringer from the date the application is published. There are two requirements: (1) the application later issues as a patent; and (2) the infringer had actual notice of the published application. (35 United States Code Sections 122, 154.) An infringer will have actual notice of a publication if he or she sees the published application. This can be accomplished by sending a copy to the infringer by certified mail.

4. Direct and Indirect Infringement

When a patent owner sues for infringement, a court must examine the patent claims, the defendant's device or process, and the defendant's actions to determine if infringement has occurred. A device or process can infringe a patent if it duplicates all of the elements in at least one patent claim ("direct infringement"). Indirect infringement can occur when someone contributes to or persuades another to infringe.

a. Direct Infringement

A defendant may commit direct infringement by either directly making, using, or selling a device or process which meets every element of a patent claim of the patented invention (called literal infringement) or by designing around the patent claims to achieve the same function in substantially the same manner and with same result. This is known as "equivalent infringement," or infringement under the "doctrine of equivalents."

In a literal infringement, the defendant's device is literally the *same* invention as that described in the patent claim. For example, a company devised an improved pH meter to measure acidity. In an attempt to recapture market share, a competitor committed literal infringement by copying the patented meter and mounting system. (*Rosemount, Inc. v. Beckman Instruments, Inc.*, 727 F.2d 1540 (Fed. Cir. 1984).)

A patent claim can specifically describe (or "recite") the function of one of the items instead of describing its structure. This type of clause is known as a means-plus-function clause (also known as a "means for" clause) because it usually starts with the word "means."

For example, a patent claim recites "a means for storing textual information" and does not specifically state any type of storage

device. In a literal infringement of a "means for" clause, a court must conduct an inquiry to determine if a storage device used in the defendant's invention is the same as or equivalent to that described in the patent's specification to support the means-plus-function clause. For example, a means for storing information could be described in the specification as a CD-ROM or floppy disc. If there's a means-plus-function clause, not all devices that meet the means plus function will infringe; only those described in the specification (or equivalents). (35 U.S.C. § 112.) Not every use of "means" will trigger this analysis. If the clause is specific enough, and the infringing device meets the "means" clause, the means-plus-function equivalency is unnecessary. (*Cole v. Kimberly-Clark Corp.*, 102 F.3d 524 (Fed. Cir. 1996).)

Even if a device is not a literal copy of a patented invention, it can be an infringement if it performs substantially the same function in substantially the same manner and obtains the same result as the patented invention. This doctrine of equivalents was created to prevent infringers from "designing around" the patent claims by making minor alterations or by using later developments that weren't available when the patent application was filed.

In 2000, a federal appeals court ruled that a patent owner could not assert any element of a patent claim in an infringement lawsuit if that element was amended (including voluntary amendments) during the patent prosecution process. In other words, the appeals court ruling, if upheld, would have barred the use of the doctrine of equivalents for any amended patent claim. In 2002, the U.S. Supreme Court struck down this absolute bar to the doctrine of equivalents and replaced it with a less arbitrary standard. Under the Supreme Court's standard, all amended claims are presumed to be narrowed so as to bar the doctrine of equivalents. But this presumption can be rebutted if a patent owner can demonstrate that the amendment involved a feature that was "unforeseeable at the time of the application" or "for some other reason" could not be included in the original claim. In that case, the patent owner can use the doctrine of equivalents. In summary, patent owners who amended their claims prior to or after the Supreme Court's decision can still use the doctrine of equivalents if they can overcome the presumption that the amendment surrendered the equivalents at issue. *Festo Corp. v. Shoketsu Kinzoku Kabushiki Co. Ltd.* 535 U.S. ___ (2002).

b. Indirect Infringement

An indirect infringement occurs when someone contributes to an infringement or persuades another to infringe. An indirect infringement cannot occur unless there is a direct infringement. It is not enough to sell infringing parts; those parts must be used in an infringing invention. For example, a company owned a patent for a device that removed sulfur from flue gas. A manufacturer sold parts to assemble the patented device without authorization. However, the manufacturer was not liable for contributory infringement because it took more than five years to construct the devices and they would not be completed until after the patent expired. (*Joy Techs. v. Flakt*, 6 F.3d 770 (Fed. Cir. 1993).)

Indirect infringement can occur in two ways: when someone is persuaded to make, use, or sell a patented invention without authorization (inducing infringement), or when a material component of a patented invention is sold with knowledge that the component is designed for an unauthorized use (contributory infringement). For example, a company patented an apparatus and method for connecting sections of metal ducts used in heating and air conditioning systems. A manufacturer was a contributory infringer because it knowingly sold the specially shaped corner pieces (that had no use other than in the patented duct connecting system) to purchasers of the patented machines. (*Met-Coil Systems Corp. v. Korners Unlimited, Inc.*, 803 F.2d 684 (Fed. Cir. 1986).)

Out of This World Infringement

Patent law states that a U.S. patent can be infringed in outer space if it is made, used, or sold in outer space on a "space object" under the jurisdiction or control of the United States.

5. Design Patent Infringement

The scope of rights of a design patent depends upon its drawings, not its claims (which merely repeat the title of the design patent). The standard for measuring design patent infringement is whether the appearance of the infringing product is "substantially the same" as the claimed design in the drawings. One standard test of this (known as the *Gorham* test) is whether an ordinary consumer finds the patented design and the imitation so similar that the resemblance is deceptive and induces consumers to purchase the imitation. For example, a musician buys a guitar mistakenly thinking that it is the patented design that he saw in a magazine.

It is also not enough that the two designs are similar; the infringing design must contain the novel features of the patented design. The novel features are the unique elements that distinguish this design from the prior art. For example, in an athletic shoes case, one company sold shoes with similar designs to another company's "Boy's Thrasher Hi-Top" shoes. The infringing shoe also included the patent's novel outer sole design. (*Avia Group International, Inc. v. L.A. Gear California*, 853 F.2d 1557 (Fed. Cir. 1988).)

A defendant accused of infringing a design patent may attempt to prove that the design patent is invalid. One common defense is to argue that the design lacks ornamentality based on the fact that the design is of no concern to consumers.

Since a design patent covers only the device's ornamental nonfunctional features, it is not an infringement to copy non-patented functional features that are associated with the design patent. For example if a musician obtains a patent on a uniquely shaped guitar knob, it is not an infringement to copy functional, non-patented elements of the knob, such as the screw-mechanism by which the knob is affixed to the guitar.

6. Activity Within U.S. Borders

A U.S. patent owner cannot stop the manufacture, use, or sale of inventions in a foreign country unless the owner has patented the invention in that country (see Chapter 9). However it is an infringement:

- to import an infringing device into the U.S., and
- to create all of the parts of a patented invention and ship those parts to a foreign company with instructions for assembly.

7. Inadvertent Infringement

For purposes of determining infringement, it doesn't matter whether a party independently develops an identical invention or inadvertently copies an invention. Any unauthorized sale, use, or manufacture qualifies as an infringement, regardless of the intent or knowledge of the defendant.

Intent and knowledge do matter for two related issues: damages and contributory infringement. The amount of money awarded to a patent owner for infringement ("damages") may vary depending on the infringer's intent. A "willful infringer," that is, someone who knew of the plaintiff's patent and deliberately infringed, may have to pay more (see Section C2). In order to be liable for contributory infringement, a company must know that the item supplied is being used to create an infringement (see Section A4).

B. Who Can Sue, Who Can Be Sued?

The patent owner can sue any manufacturer who makes, uses, sells, imports, or offers for sale any device or practices any process covered by the claims of a patent. The patent owner can sue the retailer or ultimate purchaser of the invention (including a private individual) as well as the manufacturer.

Under a theory known as vicarious liability, a business such as a corporation or partnership is liable for infringements committed by employees or agents when:

- the agent acts under the authority or direction of the business
- the employee acts within the scope of employment, or
- the business benefits, adopts or approves the infringing activity.

A company that purchases another company may be liable for infringements committed by the purchased company under a standard known as successor liability. Successor liability occurs when:

- there is an agreement between the companies to assume liability
- the two companies merge
- the purchaser is a "continuation" of the purchased business, or
- the sale is fraudulent and made to escape liability.

Because the location of the lawsuit depends on the location of the defendant (see Section C1), lawsuits against the retailer or customer are sometimes brought in order to find a court that's geographically close to the patent owner. If a suit is brought against a retailer or customer, the manufacturer of the infringing device must step in and defend or reimburse the customer's suit. If the infringer is an out-of-state manufacturer and the local retailer is sued, it places a burden on the manufacturer to defend at a distance.

⚠️ **When Governments Infringe.** The U.S. Government (or contractors making products under a government contract) can be liable for infringement if a patented invention is used or manufactured by or for the United States without authorization. However, the only remedy is financial damages and interest. The patent owner cannot obtain a court order halting the government infringement. In a 1999 decision, the Supreme Court ruled that under Constitutional principles, states couldn't be liable for patent infringement. (*Florida Prepaid Postsecondary Ed. Expense Bd. v. College Savings Bank*, 119 S. Ct. 2199 (1999).)

C. Stopping Patent Infringement

Patent laws are like stop signs along the road; people are supposed to obey them, but some do not. Often the only way to enforce patent laws is to drag the infringer into a federal court and obtain a court order prohibiting infringement and requiring the infringer to pay damages. In the following sections we discuss the elements of patent litigation and the remedies available under patent law. We discuss alternatives to patent litigation in Section E.

1. Patent Litigation

We have highlighted some common elements of patent litigation below.

a. The "Cease and Desist" or "Offer of License" Letter

The cease and desist letter is the first volley in an infringement lawsuit and accomplishes the following:

- informs the alleged infringer of the patent, that is, provides evidence of the patent's validity and ownership
- requests that infringing activity be stopped. This may or may not include a threat of litigation (see sidebar, below, When the Defendant Fires the First Shot: Declaratory Relief), and
- requests that damages or a royalty for past infringement be paid to the

patent owner. Alternatively, the patent owner can offer the infringer another option, to pay ongoing royalties and continue selling the infringing merchandise under an agreement known as a license (sometimes referred to as a "reverse license").

When the Defendant Fires the First Shot: Declaratory Relief

If a company reasonably believes that it will be sued for infringement, for example, because it received a cease and desist letter, it can sue the patent owner in a federal court for declaratory relief. This asks the court to determine the validity of the patent and whether it has been infringed. However, if the company was not reasonably threatened, for example it received an "offer to license" letter, the company has no right to file a request for declaratory judgment.

---

b. Jurisdiction and Venue

Federal district courts have the exclusive right to determine patent infringement disputes (known as "exclusive jurisdiction"). The patent owner must determine which federal court is the proper geographic location (venue) for the litigation. A lawsuit for patent infringement may be brought in the district where the defendant's residence is located, or where the defendant has committed acts of infringement and has a regular and established place of business. If the defendant is a corporation, the corporation "resides" in any district where the company is incorporated, licensed to do business, or is doing business. Lawsuits for patent infringement against the U.S. Government must be filed in the Court of Claims in Washington, D.C.

c. Complaint and Summons

The plaintiff in a patent infringement lawsuit initially prepares three documents, a complaint, a summons, and a civil cover sheet. These three documents must be filed with the federal court and delivered to the defendant under the federal court's rules of service of process.

The complaint for patent infringement sets forth the facts of the infringement and requests remedies such as compensation and injunctive relief for the infringement. (For more information about Remedies, see Section C2, below.) If the plaintiff desires a jury trial, that demand should be made in the complaint. If the plaintiff has not sought a jury trial but the defendant wants one, the request for a jury trial should be made in the defendant's answer.

d. The Answer

The answer is a response to the complaint in which the defendant admits or denies the statements and provides a list of defenses.

e. Counterclaims

If the defendant wishes to bring an action against the plaintiff, a counterclaim must be filed at the time the answer is filed. A counterclaim is compulsory. It *must* be brought if it arises out of the same transaction or occurrence that is the subject of the complaint. For example a patent owner, angry over illegal copies, assaults the president of the company making the infringements. If the patent owner sues the president for infringement, the president must assert his claim for damages for the assault in his counterclaim.

f. Discovery

Discovery is a process by which each party to the litigation acquires information for trial. The discovery may include requests for documents or may be in the form of written questions (interrogatories or requests for admissions). A party or witness may also be interviewed under oath (depositions). Discovery, especially a deposition, is extremely expensive and its cost often induces parties to settle lawsuits.

g. Protective Orders

Patent litigation often requires investigation and discovery of information that is confidential. The parties may agree to protect and limit the disclosure of such information. The court may also issue a protective order that prohibits public disclosure of the information.

h. Expert Witnesses

Often, the technical and scientific nature of patent law demands that experts in the field testify on behalf of each party. Before trial, each party identifies its expert witnesses by means of a document known as "Identification of Expert Witness."

i. Trial

The process of trying a case in front of a judge or jury is beyond the scope of this book. However, we can summarize some of the events that occur. The trial begins with opening statements from the parties followed by presentation of the plaintiff's case and then the defendant's case. Because of the large number of technical terms and scientific language, the parties often use visual aides and expert witnesses as explanatory devices. For example, the parties may simplify the procedure by creating a glossary of terms or using enlarged copies of claims or charts comparing the claims to the invention. Some attorneys use charts to illustrate the sequence of events from conception of the invention to the issuance of patents.

Each side attempts to prove the elements of its case. For example, if one side is asserting a defense, all the elements necessary to prove that defense are introduced through witnesses or through physical evidence such as documents. The witnesses for each side are cross-examined, that is, questioned by the attorneys for the opposing counsel. After each side has presented its case, the two sides summarize their positions in a final statement.

A patent case can be heard in front of a judge, or if either party elects, it can be heard in front of a jury with a judge presiding. There are some issues that a jury is not permitted to decide. For example, under a recent Supreme Court ruling, a jury may not interpret the patent claims. An interpretation may only be made by the judge. A jury may determine whether infringement has occurred and the amount of damages.

After the jury deliberates and issues a verdict, the verdict is confirmed by the judge and becomes a judgment that can be enforced by the prevailing (or winning) party. A judgment is the relief awarded by the court as the result of the judge or jury's verdict. On some occasions, the judge will set aside the jury's verdict because the judge may feel that the verdict is not supported by the law and facts.

j. Appeal

If either party is unhappy with the decision of the federal court, the case can be appealed to the United States Court of Appeals for the Federal Circuit (known as "CAFC" or the "Federal Circuit") in Washington, D.C., and which occasionally travels around the country to hear appeals. The Federal Circuit was established in order to bring about uniformity in the application of the patent laws.

A three-member panel of judges will review the trial court record to determine if a legal error occurred. If the parties are not satisfied with the Court of Appeals' determination, the only other recourse is to the U.S. Supreme Court. However, the U.S. Supreme Court rarely hears patent cases, so the CAFC's determination is usually final.

2. Remedies

A patent owner has several legal remedies for infringement. The owner can:

- obtain a court order preventing the infringing activity
- halt importation of infringing devices
- recover compensatory damages, and
- in exceptional cases, recover triple damages and attorney fees.

a. Injunctions

A court can stop all infringing activity through a written order called an injunction. The injunction can be granted at the end of a trial (a permanent injunction) or the patent owner can attempt to halt the infringing activity immediately, rather than wait for a trial. The patent owner may seek a court order halting the activity for a short period of time (known as a temporary restraining order or TRO). The TRO only lasts a few days or weeks. A temporary restraining order may be granted without notice to the infringer if it appears that immediate damage will result, for example that evidence will be destroyed.

The TRO remains in effect until the court has an opportunity to schedule a hearing for the preliminary injunction where both parties have an opportunity to present evidence. The preliminary injunction lasts until the final judgment has been rendered. Two factors are used when a court determines whether to grant a preliminary injunction. First, is the plaintiff likely to succeed in the lawsuit? Second, will the plaintiff suffer irreparable harm if the injunction is not granted? For example, the maker of a plastic cervical extrication collar was entitled to a preliminary injunction against the manufacturer of a competing plastic collar. A judge determined that the patent owner had a likelihood of success and the patent owner would suffer serious damage if sales of the infringing device were allowed to continue. (*California Med. Prods. v. Emergency Med. Prods.*, 796 F. Supp. 640 (D. R.I. 1992).)

When a TRO or preliminary injunction is issued, the court requires that the party seeking the injunction post money with the court (a bond). The bond is intended to cover the costs and damages in case the defendant prevails.

Halting Importation of Infringing Devices

If an infringing device is being imported into the U.S., the patent owner can bring a proceeding before the International Trade Commission to have the device stopped at the port of entry. This would be in addition, or as an alternative, to filing a lawsuit.

b. Compensatory Damages

A patent owner can recover money from the defendant as compensation for the damage from the infringement. These damages can be any profits lost as a result of the infringement or a royalty based upon what the patent owner would have obtained from the sale of the defendant's device. For example, a court might examine what royalties the patent owner would have received if it had licensed the defendant's sale of the infringing device. The owner of a utility patent is not entitled to the defendant's profits resulting from infringement. However, the owner of a design patent can recover the defendant's profits.

As a requirement for recovering damages, the patent owner must mark the patented device with the patent number. If the owner fails to mark the device, damages can only be recovered from the date that the patent owner notifies the infringer. Even if the patented invention is unmarked, a court can still order a halt to the sale or manufacture of the infringing device.

c. Increased Damages and Attorney Fees

In exceptional cases, financial damages may be increased, at the discretion of the court, up to triple the award (known as "enhanced damages"). In addition, a court may also award attorney's fees to the winning side. An exceptional case would be one in which infringement is willful (the defendant knew of the plaintiff's patent and deliberately infringed).

For example, a company patented a method of masking sounds and licensed the patent rights to a company. The license was later terminated but the former licensee continued to make and sell the device. On that basis, the damages were tripled and the defendant was required to pay the patent owner's attorney fees. (*Acoustical Design, Inc. v. Control Elecs. Co.*, 932 F.2d 939 (Fed. Cir. 1991).)

Some companies offer litigation insurance services. These companies will reimburse part or all of the cost of patent enforcement litigation up to the policy limit in return for an annual premium. You can even begin coverage while your patent application is pending. A business that is sued for patent infringement may also be covered under a general business liability insurance policy. Companies that offer litigation insurance include:

- Bolton/RGV Insurance Brokers, 1100 El Centro St., South Pasadena, CA 91030, 818-799-7000, ext. 375, and
- Intellectual Property Insurance Services Corp., 10503 Timberwood Circle, Louisville, KY 40223, 800-537-7863.

One company, Patent Enforcement Fund, Box L, Southport, CT 06480, 203-259-7789, will finance patent litigation in return for a partial interest in the patent.

D. Defenses to Patent Infringement

A defendant in a patent infringement law-suit usually argues that the patent owner's patent is invalid. Alternatively, it can be argued that even if it is valid, the defendant's invention does not infringe. Other defenses include arguing that the infringement is excused or that the patent owner has misused the patent or has unclean hands. Below, we examine some common patent defenses.

1. Lack of Standing

A plaintiff who doesn't own patent rights lacks the legal capacity (or "standing") to bring the lawsuit. For example, a company sues a former employee for copying a patented software program. The employee proves that he, not the software company, owns the patent. Therefore, the software company lacks standing and the case will be dismissed.

2. Patent Invalidity

A lawsuit for patent infringement almost always becomes two separate battles, one in which the plaintiff claims damage from infringement and the other in which the defendant attempts to terminate the patent rights by proving the patent is invalid. For example, in one case, the Polaroid company sued Kodak for infringement of ten instant photography patents. The court determined that Kodak infringed seven Polaroid patents; but that the other three of Polaroid's patents were invalid.

To prove that a patent is invalid, the defendant commonly attacks the patent on the basis of lack of novelty or nonobviousness. In general, all of the criteria used by the PTO to grant a patent are re-examined by the defendant at trial. The defendant will usually attempt to show prior art that anticipates or renders the patent's claims obvious or to prove that sales or disclosure of the patented invention occurred more than one year prior to filing the patent application.

For example, a company was sued for infringement of a patented device for displaying computer text on a television monitor. The defendant proved that the company had submitted a proposal for sale of the invention more than one year prior to filing its patent application. On that basis, the patent was invalidated and there was no infringement. (*RCA Corporation v. Data General Corporation*, 887 F.2d 1056 (Fed. Cir. 1989).)

3. Inequitable Conduct

A defendant may attempt to prove that a patent owner intentionally misled a patent examiner or should have known that with-held information was material (important) to the examination process. In that case, the issued patent is invalid. This defense is known as "inequitable conduct."

4. Exhaustion (First Sale Doctrine)

Once a patented item is sold, rights to that item are exhausted and it is not an infringement to resell it. This defense is known as either the "first sale exemption" or the "exhaustion doctrine." This defense does not apply if someone purchases an infringing invention, one that was initially sold without authorization from the patent owner. For example, this defense is not available if a company purchases infringing sparkplugs and resells them at retail outlets.

5. Repair Doctrine

It is not an infringement to repair a patented device and replace worn out unpatented components. It is also not contributory infringement to sell materials used to repair or replace a patented invention. This defense does not apply for completely rebuilt inventions or for unauthorized inventions, items that are made or sold without authorization from the patent owner.

For example, a company owned a patent for a convertible top apparatus used in automobiles. The fabric used in the top was not patented. Under the repair doctrine, the sale of fabric to legitimate purchasers of the patented convertible top was not an infringement or contributory infringement. However, a second company was making an infringing version of the convertible top apparatus. Any repair on these devices was an infringement. The sale of fabric for these

infringing devices was a contributory infringement. (*Aro Mfg. Co. v. Convertible Top Replacement Co.*, 365 U.S. 336 (1961).)

6. File Wrapper Estoppel

The official file in which a patent is contained at the Patent and Trademark Office is known as a "file wrapper." All statements, admissions, correspondence, or documentation relating to the invention are placed in the file wrapper. If, during the patent application process, the inventor admits limitations to the invention or disclaims certain rights, those admissions or disclaimers will become part of the file wrapper and the patent owner cannot later sue for infringement over any rights that were disclaimed in the file wrapper. This defense is known as file wrapper estoppel (or prosecution history estoppel). Estoppel means that a party is prevented from contradicting a former statement or action.

For example, a medical company owned a patent for an inflatable thermal blanket. The patent claimed a design that caused the inflated blanket to "self-erect" into a Quonset hut-like shape, preventing contact of the blanket with the patient. The prosecution history of the patent showed that the applicant relinquished rights to any forced-air blanket other than a "self-erecting" convective thermal blanket. On that basis there could not be infringement of an allegedly equivalent blanket that rested on a patient and did not inflate itself into a self-supporting structure. (*Augustine Medical Inc. v. Gaymar Industries Inc.*, 181 F.3d 1291 (Fed. Cir 1999).)

7. Regulatory Testing and Experimental Uses

To encourage competition and speed up the release of human health care and certain animal products, patent law allows companies to engage in activities that would otherwise be considered infringement if those activities were necessary for regulatory approval. If this were not available, a competitor waiting for government approval would not be able to release its product until years after a patent expires, effectively extending the patent owner's period of exclusivity.

Reverse Doctrine of Equivalents

A rarely used defense is known as the "reverse doctrine of equivalents" or "negative doctrine of equivalents." Under this defense, even if there is a literal infringement, the court will excuse the defendant's conduct if the infringing device has a different function or result than the patented invention.

8. Patent Misuse

A patent owner who has misused a patent cannot sue for infringement. Common examples of misuse are violations of the antitrust laws or unethical business practices. For example, if a patent owner conspired to fix the price of the patented item, this would violate antitrust laws. If the patent owner later sued for infringement, the defendant could argue that the owner is prohibited from suing because it has misused its patent rights.

Tying is a form of patent misuse in which, as a condition of a transaction, the buyer of a patented device must also purchase an additional product. For example, in one case, a company had a patent on a machine that deposited salt tablets in canned food. Purchasers of the machine were also required to buy salt tablets from the patent owner. The Supreme Court determined that the seller of the machine misused its patent rights and on that basis, was prevented from suing for infringement. (*Morton Salt Co. v. G.S. Suppiger Co.*, 314 U.S. 488 (1942).) In 1988, Congress enacted Patent Misuse Amendments that require that courts apply a "rule of reason" standard. Under the "rule of reason," the court must view all the relevant factors to determine if the tying arrangement is in any way justified.

9. Laches: Waiting Too Long to File the Lawsuit

There is no time limit (or statute of limitations) for filing a patent infringement lawsuit, but monetary damages can be recovered only for infringements committed during the six years prior to the filing of the lawsuit. For example, if a patent owner sues after ten years of infringement, the owner cannot recover money damages for the first four years of infringement. Despite the fact that there is no law setting a time limit, courts will not permit a patent owner to sue for infringement if the owner has waited an unreasonable amount of time to file the lawsuit (laches).

Generally, courts adopt the six-year period as being an unreasonable delay in filing the suit, unless the patent owner can provide some excuse for the delay. For example, a company owned a patent for concrete highway barriers. The company threatened litigation against a competitor but did not file the infringement lawsuit until eight years later. Since the company could not provide a reasonable basis for the delay, the case was dismissed because the company had waited too long to file the lawsuit. (*A.C. Aukerman Co. v. R.L. Chaides Construction Co.*, 960 F.2d 1020 (Fed. Cir. 1992).)

10. Defense to Method Claim Infringement

The patent laws were amended in 1999 to provide a defense that applies only to method claim patents. These patent claims cover methods of accomplishing a process, for example, the series of steps required for a software program to calculate a mutual fund investment. Anyone who created and used a process commercially at least one year before the filing date of a method claims patent has a full defense to a charge of infringement. If the defendant sold a product produced by the method before the patent's effective filing date, this will generally invalidate the patent.

The Accidental Tourist

Suppose a French airplane lands in the United States using a navigational device that is an unauthorized copy of a similar device covered by a U.S. patent. Infringement? No, because U.S. patent law permits "temporary or accidental" stops by foreign airplanes or ships containing infringing inventions, provided that the invention is used exclusively for the needs of the transporting vessel.

⚠️ **Frivolous and Fraudulent Defenses.** A defense should only be asserted if the defendant has a good faith belief that it is applicable. A defense that is completely without merit, or based upon untrue facts, can destroy the defendant's credibility and result in sanctions or imprisonment stemming from felony perjury.

E. Ending Disputes Without a Lawsuit

Patent litigation is an expensive, complex process. The American Intellectual Property Law Association estimates the median cost of patent infringement actions for each side is $280,000 up to trial, and $518,000 through trial. For that reason, many patent owners prefer to resolve infringement disputes without resorting to trial.

1. Settlement

It is possible that the infringer may wish to avoid litigation, or if litigation has started, to end it before trial. There are several advantages to a negotiated settlement:

- it saves money because there are no costs for litigation
- it saves time compared to the two to three years required for litigation, and
- it is a guaranteed payment, unlike a court judgment that must be collected and enforced.

Because of these advantages a patent owner may accept less money in settlement than demanded in a court case. When negotiating a settlement, the patent owner must consider the likelihood of prevailing in a federal court and any resulting award of damages. Sometimes, a patent owner will forego payment of damages in exchange for the infringer's agreement to halt infringement. In other cases, the patent owner may agree to permit continued manufacture or sale provided the infringer pays a royalty for all past and future sales. This is sometimes referred to as a "reverse license."

A settlement is a contract signed by both parties, usually executed at the time one party pays the other. Some states have requirements regarding settlement agreements and specific language must be included to protect the rights of the parties. Sometimes, the terms of the settlement are presented in a document that is filed with the court in a form known as a stipulated judgment.

2. Alternative Dispute Resolution

Many disputes regarding intellectual property rights are resolved privately through informal procedures known as mediation and arbitration. Mediation is a procedure in which the parties submit their dispute to an impartial mediator who assists the parties in reaching a settlement. Arbitration can be used if mediation is not successful. It is the referral of a dispute to one or more impartial persons, usually for a final and binding decision. Disputes regarding patent ownership or infringement involve technical and scientific issues and the parties may desire to have the matter decided by a person versed in the subject matter. In addition, the expense of patent litigation disfavors smaller entities. For these reasons, arbitration of patent disputes is encouraged. The American Arbitration Association has established special Patent Arbitration Rules and has gathered a national panel of patent arbitrators. International arbitration disputes are often resolved through the International Chamber of Commerce in Stockholm or the London Court of Arbitration in England. Arbitration can be initiated by an agreement or by submission of the parties.

3. Using the Re-Examination Process to Induce Settlement

The PTO can be asked to re-examine any in-force patent to determine whether prior art newly called to its attention knocks out one or more of the patent's claims. This may help the patent owner under some circumstances. For example, an infringer informs the patent owner of prior art that the infringer feels invalidates one or more claims in the patent. The patent owner (or the infringer) can request a re-examination by the PTO in light of the prior art and the PTO can issue either a certificate of patentability or unpatentability. This certificate can have a powerful effect on bringing the parties to a settlement. ∎

Chapter 9

International Patent Law

I n this chapter we explore basic principles of international patent law. Our perspective is through the eyes of the U.S. inventor. Since U.S. patent rights do not extend beyond national borders, American inventors who want to prevent foreign infringements must apply for patent rights in other countries. When applying, they rely on reciprocal patent filing rules that are part of international agreements (or treaties). These agreements provide consistent treatment for inventors in member nations. There are three important treaties that affect the rights of U.S. inventors: the Paris Convention, the Patent Cooperation Treaty (PCT), and the European Patent Convention (EPC). We will discuss these treaties and also discuss patent rights in nations that are not members of patent treaties.

A. Introduction to Foreign Patent Treaties and Laws

The owner of a U.S. patent can stop anyone from making, using, selling, or offering for sale the invention in the United States. In addition, a U.S. patent owner can stop anyone from importing unauthorized copies of the invention into the U.S. However, U.S. patent rights stop at the American border. An inventor cannot use a U.S. patent to stop someone from making, selling, or using the invention in another country. To do that, American inventors must acquire patent rights in that country and rely on rules of reciprocity in international treaties.

"Reciprocity" or "reciprocal treatment" means that when an inventor from Country A applies for a patent in Country B, the inventor will be treated in the same manner as inventors living in Country B. This reciprocal treatment extends only to inventors who live in nations that have signed the treaty ("signatory nations").

1. Patent Treaties

The U.S. is a signatory nation to several international patent treaties, the most important of which are the Paris Convention and the Patent Cooperation Treaty. A list of nations that are members of each treaty is provided in Fig. 9A at the end of this chapter. Below we provide a short synopsis of each treaty and we will provide more detail in subsequent sections.

a. Paris Convention

The U.S., like the majority of industrialized nations, is a party to the Paris Convention, an international treaty that provides reciprocal patent filing rights. Members of the Paris Convention are known as Convention countries. In order to acquire patent rights, the inventor must separately file a patent application in each Convention country. The advantage of the Paris Convention for a U.S. inventor is that the inventor's filing date can be retained in another Convention country provided that the patent application is filed in the country within one year of the U.S. filing date (or six months for design patents). For example, Roberta files her U.S. patent application on May 1, 2002. If Roberta files a patent application in Canada before May 1, 2003, she will have priority over any other patents that may have been filed after May 1, 2002.

⚠ Patent Filing in Non-Convention Countries. A U.S. inventor filing in non-Convention countries must file the foreign application before publishing or selling the invention. This is because, unlike the U.S., virtually no foreign country provides a one-year grace period (see Chapter 2, Section D). Thus, any publication or sale of the invention is fatal in foreign countries (see Section 2e, below).

b. Patent Cooperation Treaty (PCT)

Most industrialized countries are also members of the PCT, a treaty that enables inventors to file a relatively economical international application in their home country within one year of their home country filing date. There are two advantages in filing a PCT application: the inventor obtains a filing date that is good in every member country in which the inventor seeks patent protection; and an initial international patent search will be conducted and PCT member countries will rely heavily on this search. The inventor in a PCT nation must eventually file separate "national" applications in each country or group of countries (such as the EPO) where the inventor wants coverage, but the initial search procedure simplifies the international patent process.

A U.S. inventor cannot file a foreign patent application until the inventor gets a PCT foreign-filing license or until six months have elapsed from the inventor's U.S. filing date (see Section A3). The inventor can then obtain a 20- or 30-month delay, depending on whether the inventor requests examination (a provision known as "Chapter II") before filing in countries that belong to the PCT. In the following sections we will discuss these treaties and related international rules in more detail.

The High Cost of Foreign Patent Filings

Patent prosecution and practice in other countries is relatively complicated and extremely expensive. It is usually only worthwhile for U.S. inventors to file applications in a foreign country if a significant market for the invention is very likely to exist, or the inventor has a foreign licensee (someone who's paying the inventor for the invention and know-how). Otherwise, the cost of acquiring foreign patent protection may exceed the potential returns from sales of the invention. The fact that an infringement occurs in a country does not always justify filing in that country. Usually, it pays to file only if the infringement is substantial enough to justify the expense of filing, getting the patent, and the uncertainties of licensing and litigation.

c. Europatents: The European Patent Convention (EPC)

Nations that are a party to the European Economic Community (EEC) are also members of a treaty known as the European Patent Convention (EPC). For more detailed information on the EPC, see Section E.

2. The Patent Laws of Other Countries Are Different

Despite the Paris Convention and other treaties covering patent applications, and except for Canada, whose patent laws and practice are practically identical to ours, almost all countries have some differences from the U.S. in their substantive patent laws and practices. These differences have been reduced in recent years but some that still exist are as follows:

a. Opposition Proceedings After Allowance

In the U.S., once an application is examined and allowed, the patent issues without any further proceedings. However, most foreign countries have an opposition proceeding under which the application is published and anyone who believes the invention isn't patentable can cite additional prior art to the patent office in order to block the patent. The U.S. now has a procedure for publication of patent applications (see Chapter 1, Section J4), but the public may not oppose the patent.

b. Filing the Application in the Name of the Assignee

In the U.S., the patent must be applied for in the name of the actual inventor, but in most foreign countries any assignee (usually the inventor's employer-company) can apply in its own name, although the actual inventor must be named in certain countries.

c. No Novelty Examination

Many smaller countries (for example, Belgium and Portugal) don't conduct novelty examinations on applications that are filed there directly (not through the European Patent Office—EPO). Instead, they simply issue a patent on every application filed and leave it up to the courts (in the event of an infringement) to determine whether the invention was novel and nonobvious.

d. Payment of Maintenance Fees Before Issuance of Foreign Patent

Some jurisdictions (for example, the EPO, France, Germany, Italy, Australia, and Netherlands) require the payment of annual maintenance fees while the application is pending. But if the inventor files in these countries (except Australia) through the

EPO, no individual country fees are due until the Europatent issues and is registered in each country. However, annual EPO fees are due until the Europatent issues.

e. No One-Year Grace Period

Most foreign countries don't share the U.S. one-year grace period. The inventor must get an effective filing date in most countries before public release or sale of the invention. This is done either by actually filing there or by filing in the U.S. and then filing a corresponding application in Convention countries within one year. Most foreign countries consider any public release in any country as prior art, while a few recognize only public releases in their country as prior art. Some countries allow an exhibit at a recognized trade show, provided the patent application is filed in that country within six months of the exhibit or trade show.

f. Most Countries Use "First to File," Not "First to Invent" Rule

If two different inventors file respective patent applications on the same invention, most countries will award a patent to the "first to file," a simple, economical, and easy-for-a-layperson system. However, the U.S. and the Philippines award the patent to the "first to invent," a system that requires an expensive, complicated, and lawyer-conducted trial proceeding called an interference (see Chapter 6, Section C).

g. Expenses and Difficulties in the Japanese Patent Process

In Japan, the filing and translation fees are very high. Then, examination must be separately requested within seven years, requiring another stiff fee. After examination is requested, it takes about three years before the Japanese Patent Office, which is understaffed, gets around to it. Getting the application allowed is very difficult. However, it will be given more respect than in the U.S. Competitors will be far less likely to infringe or challenge it. Nevertheless, Japanese courts tend to interpret patents narrowly. Claims are not given a broad reading. The result is that it is possible to make small variations to the claims of a patent and avoid infringement.

3. The Early Foreign Filing License or Mandatory Six-Month Delay

Normally, after filing a U.S. application, the inventor receives a blue filing receipt from the PTO that permits the inventor to file abroad. This permission will usually be printed on the inventor's filing receipt as follows: "Foreign Filing License Granted 2002 Aug 9." However, if the inventor's filing receipt fails to include a foreign filing license (only inventions with possible military applications won't include the license), the inventor isn't allowed to file in foreign countries until six months following the inventor's U.S. filing date. What's the reason for this? To give the U.S. government a chance to review the inventor's application for possible classification on national security grounds.

Few inventors are affected by any of this, as most applications get the foreign filing license immediately. In any case, there is usually no good reason to file before six months after the inventor's U.S. filing. If the invention does have military applications, the inventor will not only fail to get a foreign filing license, but may receive a Secrecy Order from the PTO requiring that the inventor keep the invention secret until it's declassified. This often takes 12 years. The inventor's patent can't issue until then, but the Government may compensate the inventor if they use the invention in the meantime. The inventor can foreign file an application that is under a Secrecy Order. Nonetheless, it's complicated and requires assistance from a patent attorney experienced in this area.

before seeking patent protection. The most common approach taken by U.S. inventors seeking global patent rights is listed below. In subsequent sections we will explain each of the procedures.

1. First, file in the U.S and then file in non-Convention countries before publication or sale of the invention.
2. Within one year, under the Paris Convention, file a PCT application to cover PCT countries and jurisdictions (including the EPO).
3. Select the PTO or EPO for purposes of the patent search.
4. Within 19 months from the inventor's U.S. filing date, elect Chapter II of the PCT to get the application examined, either in the PTO or EPO.
5. Within 30 months from the U.S. filing date, file national applications, usually with the assistance of foreign patent agents, in the EPO and non-EPO PCT countries.

B. Putting It Together: The Most Common Route for U.S. Inventors Seeking Foreign Patent Coverage

As noted, the cost of acquiring foreign patent protection may exceed the potential return from the sale of the invention in a country (see sidebar, above, The High Cost of Foreign Patent Filings). Inventors are advised to analyze the commercial potential of an invention within a foreign nation

C. The Paris Convention and the One-Year Foreign Filing Rule

The International Convention for the Protection of Industrial Property (known as the Paris Convention or simply "the Convention") is the oldest international patent treaty. The United States is a "Convention country," as are countries of the EPO, PCT, and AIPO (the African Intellectual Property Organization). A table listing Convention countries is provided in Fig. 9A at the end of this chapter.

Treaty Members: Jurisdiction and Nations

As with many international treaties, members of the Paris Convention do not have to be an individual country, but may be an organization or group of countries. For example, the EPO is considered a separate signatory of the Paris Convention. For this reason, these treaties often refer to members as "member jurisdictions," rather than as member nations or countries.

A U.S. inventor who files a regular patent application or provisional patent application (PPA, discussed in Chapter 3, Section E), can file a patent application in any Convention country within one year of the inventor's earliest filing date (or within six months for designs). The inventor's application in the Convention country will be entitled to the filing date of the inventor's U.S. application for purposes of prior-art examinations.

EXAMPLE: Sam files a regular patent application in the U.S. on 2002 September 1. Within one year he files French, Spanish, German, Brazilian, and Australian patent applications and is entitled to the filing date of 1 September 2002 in these countries.

Each Convention filing must be made in the language of the country in which the coverage is sought, except in the EPO, where a U.S. applicant can use English. Separate filing and search fees must be paid in each country. Many members of the Paris Convention also belong to the PCT (see Fig. 9A at the end of this chapter). Filing patent applications in countries that belong to both the Paris Convention and the PCT is generally easier than filing in non-PCT Convention countries.

If the inventor fails to file any foreign applications within the one-year period, the inventor can still file after the one-year period in any foreign countries, provided the inventor hasn't sold, published, or patented the invention yet.

However, if the inventor misses the Convention's one-year deadline:

- the inventor's foreign application won't be entitled to the filing date of the inventor's original application, and
- any such late application won't get the benefit of the inventor's original U.S. filing date, so any relevant prior art that has been published in the meantime can be applied against the inventor's application.

Don't Miss the One-Year Filing Deadline. If the inventor misses the one-year Paris Convention deadline and the PTO subsequently issues the U.S. patent, it's too late to file a foreign application *anywhere*! The inventor will acquire patent rights only in the U.S.

Other International Treaties

There are three other international treaties with rules similar to the Paris Convention. Members of these treaties have reciprocal priority rights in each other's countries. For example, the U.S. has entered into treaties with China-Taiwan, India, and Thailand. Inventors who file a U.S. application can file patent applications in each of these countries within one year and obtain the benefit of their U.S. filing date, and vice versa. Members of these treaties are listed in Fig. 9A at the end of this chapter.

Filing in Non-Convention Countries

Fig. 9A identifies countries that are not members of the Paris Convention. U.S. inventors can file in these countries at any time, provided:

- the invention hasn't yet become publicly known, either by the inventor's publication, by patenting, by public sale or by normal publication, in the course of prosecution in a foreign country, and
- the inventor has been given a foreign-filing license on the inventor's U.S. filing receipt (see Section D1) or six months have elapsed from the inventor's U.S. filing date.

D. The Patent Cooperation Treaty (PCT)

The PCT is administered by the World Intellectual Property Organization in Geneva. Under the Patent Cooperation Treaty (PCT), the inventor can file a patent application in the U.S. and then file a single "international application" (the "PCT application") with the PCT Department of the PTO that establishes a filing date for all member countries (see Section 1, below). This filing does not result in a universal PCT patent; the inventor must eventually file separate or "national" applications in each PCT jurisdiction (see Section 3, below). However, the PCT application provides the following advantages:

- By filing one PCT application, the inventor obtains a filing date that is good in every member country in which the inventor seeks patent protection.
- An initial international patent search will be conducted by the PTO on the PCT application and member countries will rely heavily on this search. This saves a great deal of expense and delay that would result if separate searches were conducted in each country.
- The inventor does not have to decide whether to file in individual member countries until 20 or 30 months (depending on whether the applicant elects a process known as "Chapter II"—see below) after the filing date in the original country.

If the inventor desires patent coverage in a PCT country, the PCT application must be translated for non-English-speaking jurisdictions. It also must be filed in the foreign country within 20 months after the inventor's U.S. filing or priority date, or eight months after the inventor's date of filing the PCT application in the U.S., if the PCT application is filed one year after the priority date.

The period for entering the national stage can be extended from 20 to 30 months if, within 19 months of the U.S. filing date, the inventor elects a PCT procedure known as "Chapter II" which is a request for a full examination by the PTO or the EPO (see Section D). Note, not all PCT jurisdictions allow a Chapter II procedure (see Fig. 9A).

If the inventor elects Chapter II, the inventor can wait up to 30 months to make these separate filings in foreign jurisdictions. After filing the PCT application, the inventor will receive a "search report." The inventor can then amend the claims once and submit a brief statement responding to any issues raised by the report. If the inventor continues with Chapter II, the inventor can prosecute and amend the patent claims after the examination is made. The inventor eventually receives a formal indication of allowability (or rejection) from the examiner.

Before 30 months (whether or not the application is allowed or rejected), the inventor can file the application in any PCT jurisdiction. It will again be examined and eventually either issued as a patent or rejected. A list of the PCT jurisdictions is given in Fig. 9A. All PCT members are members of the Paris Convention, but not vice versa.

For additional assistance filing a PCT application, consult *Patent It Yourself*, by attorney David Pressman (Nolo), or review *The PCT Applicant's Guide* from the PCT Department of the PTO or the PCT section of the PTO's website. Information regarding a country's patent laws may be obtained from the country's consulate office in the U.S.

1. Preparing an International Application Under the PCT

To file a PCT application, the inventor prepares the original U.S. application and drawings on A4 size paper. The main differences between the PCT and U.S. national formats (both of which are acceptable for U.S. applications) are the drawing size and margins, location of page numbers, and spacing between typed lines. (The standards are detailed in Chapter 5, Section E.)

In addition to the PCT application, a "Request" form (PTO PCT/RO/101) and a "transmittal letter" (Form PTO 1382) are required. Both forms are available from the PTO website or from Box PCT, Assistant Commissioner for Patents, Washington, DC 20231, Phone: 703-305-3257, Fax: 703-305-3230. The inventor must also pay fees, which are listed at the PTO's website, www.uspto.gov.

After completing the forms, the inventor requests a certified copy of the inventor's U.S. application for use with the PCT application, or it can be ordered on the Request form mentioned earlier. A copy of the inventor's application in PCT (A4) format (with drawings) is attached and these materials and payment of fees are mailed to: Box PCT, Assistant Commissioner for Patents, Washington, DC 20231, which is a designated receiving office for the International Bureau. It is advisable to file the PCT application at least a month before the anniversary of the inventor's U.S. filing date. However, the inventor can mail the PCT application as late as the last day of the one-year period from the inventor's U.S. filing date if the inventor uses Express Mail and completes the Express Mail Certification on page 1 of the transmittal letter.

The inventor will receive a filing receipt and separate serial number for the international PCT application. The application will eventually be transmitted for filing to the countries (including the EPO) designated on the inventor's Request form. If the inventor makes any minor errors in the PCT application, the PCT Department of the PTO will give the inventor a month to correct them. When the inventor receives the PCT search report (either from the PTO or EPO), the inventor can comment on it and amend the inventor's claims once if desired, but no extended prosecution or negotiation is permitted.

2. Chapter II of the PCT

Within 19 months of the inventor's U.S. filing date, the inventor can elect Chapter II. This requires selecting either the PTO or the EPO to examine the application. If the inventor selects the EPO to do the examination, the inventor must file the papers with the EPO in Munich and pay the fee in Deutschmarks. The inventor will receive an examination report indicating which claims will actually be allowed or rejected. The inventor can amend the application once and even interview the inventor's examiner. The relative advantages of the EPO are discussed in Section E. A list of countries that have accepted Chapter II is provided in Fig. 9A.

3. National Filings Under the PCT

If Chapter II was elected, the inventor must file a national application in each country or jurisdiction in the inventor's PCT application within 30 months from the inventor's U.S. filing date. As mentioned, each of the separate countries and the EPO will rely to a great extent on the international examination received as part of the PCT process. In most cases this examination will be based upon the EPO patent search or adopted from the U.S. patent search. This is one advantage of the PCT approach because the inventor saves money and time by not having to separately and fully prosecute an application in each country in which the inventor elected to file.

Filing in Non-PCT Convention Countries

If a U.S. inventor desires to file in a Convention country that is not a member of the PCT, the inventor must use a patent agent, a patent expert licensed to file under that non-Convention country's patent laws. The requirements vary from country to country, but special drawings in each country's format will always be needed. The inventor's foreign agent can prepare these or the inventor can have these prepared by companies that make drawings for U.S. divisional applications (see discussion of "Divisional Applications" in Chapter 6, Section C).

The foreign agent will require a power of attorney (sometimes notarized) and a certified copy of the inventor's U.S. application that can be obtained from the PTO. The cost for filing a foreign application in each individual country is about $1,000 to $5,000, depending on the country, the length of the inventor's application, and whether a translation is required. Information about locating a foreign patent agent is provided in Section F.

Don't Procrastinate. A U.S. inventor should make foreign filing decisions and take action about two or three months before the end of any of the filing periods described in this chapter. This is to give the inventor and the foreign agents time to prepare (or have prepared) the necessary correspondence and translations and to order a certified copy, if needed, of the inventor's U.S. application. Although the inventor shouldn't wait until the very end of the one-year period, the inventor also shouldn't file until near the end, since there's no advantage in filing early, unless the inventor needs an early patent—for example, because the inventor is concerned about ongoing foreign infringements.

E. European Patent Office (EPO)

The European Patent Office (EPO) is a trilingual patent office in Munich, Germany, created as a result of a treaty known as the European Patent Convention (EPC). The EPO grants "Europatents" that are good in all member countries. An inventor can make one patent filing in the EPO and if a Europatent is issued, the patentee can then register and file translations of the patent in whatever individual member countries the patentee has selected. The patent office in each EPC country does not have to review the application separately. Unless the inventor is a resident of one of the EPO-member countries, the inventor must file in the EPO via a European patent agent.

There is an additional advantage for filing at the EPO. The European Patent Convention is considered the same as a single country (a jurisdiction) under the Paris Convention and the PCT. Therefore, a U.S. inventor can file at the EPO and the effective filing date will be the same as the inventor's original U.S. filing date (provided the application is filed within the one-year foreign filing rule discussed in Section C).

Although quite rigorous, the examination procedure at the EPO is generally smoother than the PTO because the examiners are better trained (all speak and write three languages fluently) and because they take the initiative and suggest how to write the inventor's claims to get them allowed. The EPO application is published for opposition 18 months after filing. During the pendency of the EPO application, an annual mainte-nance fee must be paid to the EPO.

If the inventor's application is allowed, the inventor is granted a Europatent that lasts for 20 years from the inventor's filing date (provided the inventor pays maintenance fees in the selected member countries). The patent is automatically valid in each member country of the EPC that is designated in the inventor's application, provided that the inventor registers, files translations, and appoints an agent in each country. All member countries of the EPO are indicated in Fig. 9A, below.

There are some drawbacks for U.S. inven-tors. Filing in the EPO is very expensive and requires payment of an annuity to the EPO each year the inventor's application is on file there, until the Europatent issues. If the inventor registers the patent in any EPC member country, the inventor must pay annuities in that country.

F. Locating Foreign Patent Agents

U.S. inventors who want to file abroad will probably need to find a foreign patent agent who's familiar with patent prosecution in the countries where protection is desired. In most countries, patent professionals are called "agents" rather than attorneys. As in the U.S., foreign agents are licensed to represent clients before their patent office, but not their courts.

One method of locating a foreign agent is through a U.S. patent attorney (see Chap-ter 10) since most attorneys are associated with one or more patent agents in other countries. Names of agents can also be lo-cated:

- in the telephone directory of the city where the patent office of the foreign country is located
- at the consulate of the country (most foreign countries have consulates in major U.S. cities)
- in the Martindale-Hubbell Law Direc-tory (www.martindalehubbell.com), which lists some foreign patent attor-neys in each country (use the search engine at http://lawyers.martindale.com/Executable/Location.php3 and choose the country and "intellectual property" as practice area)
- for purpose of filing in Europe, by hiring a British firm of patent agents to do all EPO filings or hiring a Ger-man firm of patent agents in Munich.

Country or Jurisdiction	Paris Cnvn.	EPO	PCT	Pan Am Cnvn.
Albania	■		■	
Algeria	■		■	
Antigua & Barbuda	■		■	
Argentina	■			
ARIPO *	■		■	
Armenia°	■		■	
Australia	■		■	
Austria	■	■	■	
Azerbaijan°	■		■	
Bangladesh	■			
Barbados	■		■	
Belarus°	■		■	
Belgium	■	■	■	
Belize	■		■	
Bolivia	■			
Bosnia-Herzegovina	■		■	
Brazil	■		■	
Bulgaria	■		■	
Burundi	■			
Canada	■		■	
Chile	■			
China, Mainland[1]	■		■	
China, Taiwan△				
Colombia	■		■	
Congo	■			
Costa Rica	■		■	■
Côte d'Ivoire	■			
Croatia	■		■	
Cuba	■		■	
Cyprus	■	■	■	
Czech Republic	■		■	
Denmark	■	■	■	
Dominica	■		■	
Dominican Republic	■			
Ecuador	■		■	■
Egypt	■			
El Salvador	■			
Equatorial Guinea	■		■	
Estonia	■		■	
Ethiopia				
European Pat. Off.	■	■	■	
Finland	■	■	■	
France	■	■	■	
Gambia	■		■	
Georgia	■		■	
Germany	■	■	■	
Ghana	■		■	
Greece	■	■	■	
Grenada	■			
Grenadines	■		■	
Guatemala	■			■
Guinea-Bissau	■			
Guyana	■			
Haiti	■			
Holy See	■			
Honduras	■			
Hungary	■		■	
Iceland	■		■	
India△	■		■	
Indonesia	■		■	
Iran	■			
Iraq	■			
Ireland	■	■	■	
Israel	■		■	
Italy	■	■	■	
Jamaica	■			
Japan	■		■	
Jordan	■			
Kazakhstan°	■		■	
Korea, North	■		■	

⚠ The PCT organization (WIPO) is a member of the Paris Convention.

* African Regional Industrial Property Organization: Ghana, Kenya, Malawi, Sudan, and Uganda.

° Also can be covered by Eurasian Patent from Eurasian Patent Office in Moscow.

[1] Includes Hong Kong

△ Separate priority treaties between United States and Taiwan, India, and Thailand.

† African Intellectual Property Organization: Common patent system for French-speaking African countries: Benin, Burkina Faso, Cameroon, Central African Republic, Chad, Congo, Côte d'Ivoire, Gabon, Guinea, Mali, Mauritania, Niger, Senegal, and Togo.

Figure 9A—Memberships in Patent Conventions

Country or Jurisdiction	Paris Cnvn.	EPO	PCT	Pan Am Cnvn.
Korea, South	■		■	
Kuwait				
Kyrgyzstan°	■		■	
Lao Dem. Rep.	■			
Latvia	■		■	
Lebanon	■			
Lesotho	■		■	
Liberia	■		■	
Libya	■			
Liechtenstein	■	■	■	
Lithuania	■		■	
Luxembourg	■	■	■	
Macedonia	■		■	
Madagascar	■		■	
Malaysia	■			
Malta	■			
Mauritania	■		■	
Mauritius	■			
Mexico	■		■	
Moldova, Republic of	■		■	
Monaco	■	■	■	
Mongolia	■		■	
Morocco	■		■	
Mozambique	■		■	
Netherlands	■	■	■	
New Zealand	■		■	
Nicaragua	■			■
Niger	■		■	
Nigeria	■			
Norway	■		■	
OAPI †	■		■	
Oman	■		■	
Pakistan				
Panama	■			
Papua New Guinea	■			
Paraguay	■			
Peru	■			
Philippines	■		■	
Poland	■		■	
Portugal	■	■	■	

Country or Jurisdiction	Paris Cnvn.	EPO	PCT	Pan Am Cnvn.
Qatar	■			
Romania	■		■	
Russian Federation°	■		■	
Rwanda	■			
St. Kitts & Nevis	■			
Saint Lucia	■		■	
San Marino	■			
Sierra Leone	■		■	
Singapore	■		■	
Slovakia	■		■	
Slovenia	■		■	
South Africa	■		■	
Spain	■	■	■	
Sri Lanka	■		■	
Sudan	■			
Suriname	■			
Swaziland	■		■	
Sweden	■	■	■	
Switzerland	■	■	■	
Syria	■			
Tajikistan°	■		■	
Tanzania	■		■	
Thailand△				
Togo	■		■	
Tonga	■			
Trinidad & Tobago	■		■	
Tunisia	■			
Turkey	■	■	■	
Turkmenistan°	■		■	
Ukraine	■		■	
United Arab Emirates	■		■	
United Kingdom	■	■	■	
United States	■		■	
Uruguay	■			
Uzbekistan	■		■	
Venezuela	■			
Vietnam	■		■	
Yugoslavia	■		■	
Zambia	■			
Zimbabwe	■		■	

Figure 9A—Memberships in Patent Conventions (continued)

Although perhaps not as fluent in English as their British counterparts, these agents have the compensating advantage of their physical proximity to the EPO, Also, consult the listing of registered patent agents and European law firms at the EPO's page of website links (www.european-patent-office.org/online)

• conducting an Internet search for suitable patent agents; those who have websites can be located easily by using search terms like "Japanese patent agent."

Foreign Patent Agents. If possible, seek references or background information regarding the services of a foreign patent agent. In addition, seek a written estimate of the expected costs. Some foreign patent agents, like some U.S. patent attorneys and agents, are not competent or are inclined to overcharge. ∎

Chapter 10

Help Beyond This Book

Hopefully, this book provides all the basic information you will need. However, you may find yourself in a complicated situation that will require additional research or professional advice from a patent attorney or other expert. We have provided some additional resources in this chapter if you do have to get outside help.

In Section A, we direct you to sources of more information for inventors. In Section B, we provide additional resources on patents and intellectual property law. Section C offers guidance on working with attorneys.

A. Inventor Resources

The following is a list of inventor resources, including organizations, bookstores, and websites with special information on patents and other intellectual property issues.

- **Intellectual Property Creators** (www. heckel.org). The IPC provides a helpful site to learn about inventor policy issues and patent enforcement.
- **Inventor's Bookstore** (www. inventorhelp.com). The Inventor's Bookstore offers condensed reports and other guidance for inventors.
- *Inventors' Digest* (www. inventorsdigest.com). The *Inventors' Digest* and its accompanying website publish information for independent inventors at a subscription rate of $27/year for six issues. It includes articles on new inventions, licensing,

and marketing, and advertisements from reputable inventor promotion companies.

- **National Inventor Fraud Center** (www. inventorfraud.com). This organization reports on fraud by invention marketing companies.
- **National Technology Transfer Center** (NTTC) (www.nttc.edu). The NTTC at Wheeling Jesuit University helps entrepreneurs and companies looking to access federally funded research and development activity at American universities. Write to 316 Washington Avenue, Wheeling, WV 26003. Phone: 800-678-6882. Fax: 304-243-4388. Email: technology@nttc.edu.
- **Patent It Yourself** (www.patentityourself.com). Patent information and updates for David Pressman's *Patent It Yourself* (Nolo).
- **PTO Independent Inventor Resources** (www.uspto.gov/web/offices/com/ iip/indextxt.htm). In 1999, the PTO established a new office aimed at providing services and support to independent inventors. This office is expected to eventually offer seminars and expanded educational opportunities for inventors. Phone: 800-PTO-9199 or 703-308-HELP.
- **Ronald J. Riley's Inventor Resources** (www.inventored.org). This website provides comprehensive links and advice for inventors.
- **The Patent Cafe** (www.patentcafe.com). An inventor resource maintained by in-

ventor and entrepreneur Andy Gibbs. It lists inventor organizations and related links and provides information on starting an inventor organization.

- **Source Translation and Optimization Patent Website** (www.bustpatents.com). A source of information on questionable patents and patent practices by one of the PTO's most vocal critics. Also offers a free newsletter.

- **United Inventors Association (UIA).** A national inventor's organization. Write to P.O. Box 23447, Rochester, NY 14692-3347. Phone: 716-359-9310. Fax: 716-359-1132. Email: UIAUSA@aol.com.

B. Patents and Intellectual Property Resources

Provided below are some additional sources of information on patent and intellectual property law. Many of these sources are accessible through the Internet.

1. Nolo Books on Intellectual Property

There is a world of intellectual property law beyond patents. If you are interested in understanding other principles of intellectual property law that may apply to your invention, Nolo.com, the publisher of this book, also publishes a number of other titles on intellectual property, including:

- *Copyright Your Software*, by Stephen Fishman.
- *Nondisclosure Agreements: Protect Your Trade Secrets and More*, by Richard Stim and Stephen Fishman.
- *Patent It Yourself*, by David Pressman.
- *Patent, Copyright and Trademark: A Desk Reference to Intellectual Property Law*, by Stephen Elias and Richard Stim.
- *The Copyright Handbook*, by Stephen Fishman.
- *The Inventor's Notebook*, by Fred Grissom and David Pressman.
- *Trademark: Legal Care for Your Business and Product Name*, by Stephen Elias.
- *How to Make Patent Drawings Yourself*, by Jack Lo and David Pressman.
- *Patent Searching Made Easy*, by David Hitchcock.
- *Web and Software Development: A Legal Guide*, by Stephen Fishman.

2. Additional Intellectual Property Resources

- **U.S. Copyright Office.** The Copyright Office has numerous circulars, kits, and other publications that can help you, including one on searching copyright records. These publications and application forms can be obtained by writing to the Copyright Office at Publications Section, LM-455, Copyright Office, Library of Congress, Washington, DC 20559.

Most Copyright Office publications can be downloaded at www.loc. gov/copyright. Frequently requested circulars and announcements are also available via the Copyright Office's fax-on-demand telephone line at 202-707-9100.

- **Government Printing Office** (www.access.gpo.gov/#info). The Government Printing Office website is a searchable source for U.S. Code of Federal Regulations, *Congressional Record,* and other Government Printing Office products and information.

- **Intellectual Property Mall** (www.ipmall.fplc.edu). Franklin Pierce Law Center's Intellectual Mall provides IP links and information.

- **Legal Information Institute** (http:// lii.law.cornell.edu). The Legal Information Institute provides intellectual property links and downloadable copies of statutes and cases.

- **U.S. Patent & Trademark Office (PTO): Patent Information** (www.uspto.gov). The PTO website offers a number of informational pamphlets. There is also an alphabetical and geographical listing of patent attorneys and agents registered to practice before the PTO ("Directory of Registered Patent Attorneys and Agents Arranged by States and Countries"). The PTO also has an online searchable database of patent abstracts (short summaries of patents). For purposes of patent

searching, this database is an excellent and inexpensive first step in the searching procedure. Most patent forms can be downloaded from the PTO website as well as many important publications, including *General Information About Patents, Manual of Patent Examining Procedures, Examination Guidelines for Computer-Related Inventions, and Disclosure Document Program.* A PTO products and services catalog is also available. Phone: 800-PTO-9199.

- **Trade Secrets Home Page** (www.execpc.com/~mhallign). The website includes explanations of trade secret law online and current trade secret news.

- **U.S. Patent & Trademark Office (PTO): Trademark Information.** Trademarks are examined and registered by a division of the PTO. *General Information About Trademarks*, an introductory pamphlet about trademarks, and other information about the operations of the Patent and Trademark Office is available from the Superintendent of Documents, Government Printing Office, Washington, DC 20402, or from the PTO's website at www. uspto.gov. This site also includes the relevant applications and trademark office forms. You can also write to the Assistant Commissioner for Trademarks, 2900 Crystal Drive, Arlington, VA 22202-3515.

- **U.S. Code** (http://uscode.house.gov/usc.htm). This website is a source for the United States Code, which includes copyright, trademark, and patent laws.
- **Yahoo Intellectual Property Directory** (www.yahoo.com/Government/Law/Intellectual_Property). The Yahoo Intellectual Property Directory is a thorough listing of intellectual property resources on the Internet.
- *The PCT Applicant's Guide*, a brochure on how to utilize the PCT, is available for free from the PCT Department of the U.S. Patent & Trademark Office. PCT information and software for facilitating completion of the PCT forms is available through the PTO's website (www.uspto.gov). It is also available from the World Intellectual Property Organization (WIPO), Post Office Box 18, 1211 Geneva 20, Switzerland, and on the PCT's website (www.wipo.int).

Nolo's website (www.nolo.com) also offers an extensive Legal Encyclopedia that includes a section on intellectual property. You'll find answers to frequently asked questions about patents, copyrights, trademarks and other related topics, as well as sample chapters of Nolo books and a wide range of articles. Simply click "Legal Encyclopedia" and then "Patent, Copyright & Trademark."

Legal Research: You Can Do It

Conducting legal research is not as difficult as it may seem. Nolo publishes a basic legal research guide, *Legal Research: How to Find and Understand the Law*, written by attorneys Stephen Elias and Susan Levinkind. It walks you through the various sources of law, explains how they fit together and shows you how to use them to answer your legal question. *Legal Research* also directs you to legal information available on the Internet.

For detailed legal research, you will probably have to visit a local law library. If there's a public law school in your area, it probably has a law library that's open to the public. Other public law libraries are often run by local bar associations or as an adjunct to the local courts. Law libraries associated with private law schools often allow only limited public access. Call to speak with the law librarian to determine your right to access. You can always call your local bar association to find out what public law libraries are in your area.

C. Working With an Attorney

At some point, you may need the advice and counsel of an experienced patent attorney. Your first step is to find one in your area who can help you. All patent attorneys are listed in the PTO publication, *Attorneys and Agents Registered to Practice Before the U.S. Patent and Trademark Office* (A&ARTP). It is available in many public libraries and Patent and Trademark Depository Libraries, government bookstores and on the PTO's website (www.uspto.gov).

The American Intellectual Property Law Association (AIPLA) may be able to assist you in locating patent attorneys in your area. Contact the AIPLA at http://www.aipla.org or at 2001 Jefferson Davis Highway, Suite 203, Arlington, VA 22202, phone: 703-415-0780. The Intellectual Property Law Association of the American Bar Association also has a listing of intellectual property attorneys. Contact them at www.abanet.org or at 312-988-5000.

Most attorneys bill on an hourly basis ($150 to $300 an hour) and send a bill at the end of each month. Some attorneys bill on a fixed fee basis. For example, $400 for a patent validity opinion, $800 for a patent-ability search, and $400 for a simple patent application.

In many states, such as California, a client always has the right to terminate the attorney, although this does not terminate the obligation to pay the attorney. If you don't respect and trust your attorney's professional abilities, you should switch and find a new attorney. Under most state bar rules, your attorney is required to deliver all of your papers to you at your request upon termination. However, you should not make this decision hastily. Switching attorneys is a nuisance and you may lose time and money. For more information on how to handle a dispute with your lawyer, see *Mad at Your Lawyer*, by attorney Tanya Starnes (Nolo).

Reducing the Size of Your Bill

Working with a patent attorney can be expensive. You can save yourself a lot of money and grief by following this list of helpful tips as you work through your case.

Keep it short. If you are paying your attorney on an hourly basis, keep your conversations short and avoid making several calls a day. Consolidate your questions so that you can ask them all in one conversation.

Get a fee agreement. We recommend that you get a written fee agreement when dealing with an attorney. Read it and understand your rights as a client. Make sure that your fee agreement gives you the right to an itemized statement along with the bill detailing the work done and time spent. Some state statutes and bar associations require a written fee agreement; for example, California requires that attorneys provide a written agreement when the fee will exceed $1000.

Review billings carefully. Your lawyer's bill should be clear. Do not accept summary billings such as the single phrase "litigation work" used to explain a block of time for which you are billed a great deal of money.

Watch out for hidden expenses. Find out what expenses you must cover. Watch out if your attorney wants to bill for services such as word processing or administrative services. This means you will be paying the secretary's salary. Also beware of fax and copying charges. Some firms charge clients per page for incoming and outgoing faxes.

Don't take litigation lightly. As a general rule, beware of litigation! If you are involved in a lawsuit, it may take months or years to resolve. Some go on for decades. It usually costs $100,000 or more and the only ones who profit are usually the lawyers. The average cost for a full-blown patent infringement suit is now about $300,000. If you're in a dispute, ask your attorney about alternative dispute resolution (ADR) methods such as arbitration and mediation. Often these procedures can save money and they're faster than litigation. If those methods don't work or aren't available, ask your attorney for an assessment of your odds and the potential costs before filing a lawsuit. The assessment and underlying reasoning should be in plain English. If a lawyer can't explain your situation clearly to you, he probably won't be able to explain it clearly to a judge or jury.

 For information on monitoring a lawsuit, read *The Lawsuit Survival Guide: A Client's Companion to Litigation,* by Joseph L. Matthews (Nolo).

Patent Glossary

abstract a concise, one-paragraph summary of the patent. It details the structure, nature, and purpose of the invention. The abstract is used by the PTO and the public to quickly determine the gist of what is being disclosed.

actual damages (also known as compensatory damages) in a lawsuit, money awarded to one party to cover actual injury or economic loss. Actual damages are intended to put the injured party in the position he was in prior to the injury.

answer a written response to a complaint (the opening papers in a lawsuit) in which the defendant admits or denies the allegations and may provide a list of defenses.

best mode the inventor's principal and preferred method of embodying the invention.

Board of Appeals and Patent Interferences (BAPI) a tribunal of judges at the PTO that hears appeals from final Office Actions.

cease and desist letter correspondence from the owner of a proprietary work that requests the cessation of all infringing activity.

clear and convincing proof evidence that is highly probable and free from serious doubt.

complaint papers filed with a court clerk by the plaintiff to initiate a lawsuit by setting out facts and legal claims (usually called causes of action).

compositions of matter items such as chemical compositions, conglomerates, aggregates, or other chemically significant substances that are usually supplied in bulk (solid or particulate), liquid, or gaseous form.

conception the mental part of inventing, including how an invention is formulated or how a problem is solved.

confidentiality agreement (also known as a nondisclosure agreement) a contract in which one or both parties agree not to disclose certain information.

continuation application a new patent application that allows the applicant to re-present an invention and get a second or third bite at the apple. The applicant can file a new application (known as a "continuation") while the original (or "parent") application is still pending. A continuation application consists of the same invention, cross-referenced to the parent application and a new set of claims. The applicant retains the filing date of the parent application for purposes of determining the relevancy of prior art.

Continuation-In-Part (CIP) less common than a continuation application, this form of extension application is used when a portion or all of an earlier patent application is continued and new matter (not disclosed in the earlier application) is included. CIP applications are used when an applicant wants to present an improvement but is prevented from adding a pending application to it because of the prohibition against adding "new matter."

Continuing Prosecution Application (CPA) a patent application that is like a continuation application in effect, but no new application need be filed. The applicant merely pays another filing fee, submits new claims, and files a CPA request form. CPAs can only be used for applications filed prior to 2000 May 29. Applications after that date must use the Request for Continued Examination.

contributory infringement occurs when a material component of a patented invention is sold with knowledge that the component is designed for an unauthorized use. This type of infringement cannot occur unless there is a direct infringement. In other words, it is not enough to sell infringing parts; those parts must be used in an infringing invention.

copyright the legal right to exclude others, for a limited time, from copying, selling, performing, displaying, or making derivative versions of a work of authorship such as a writing, music, or artwork.

counterclaim a legal claim usually asserted by the defendant against an opposing party, usually the plaintiff.

Court of Appeals for the Federal Circuit (CAFC) the federal appeals court that specializes in patent appeals. If the Board of Appeals and Patent Interferences rejects an application appeal, an applicant can further appeal to the CAFC within 60 days of the decision. If the CAFC upholds the PTO, the applicant can request the United States Supreme Court hear the case (although the Supreme Court rarely hears patent appeals).

date of invention the earliest of the following dates: (a) the date an inventor filed the patent application (provisional or regular), (b) the date an inventor can prove that the invention was built and tested in the U.S. or a country that is a member of North American Free Trade Association (NAFTA) or the World Trade Organization (WTO), or (c) the date an inventor can prove that the invention was conceived in a NAFTA or WTO country, provided the inventor can also prove diligence in building and testing it or filing a patent application on it.

declaratory relief a request that the court sort out the rights and legal obligations of the parties in the midst of an actual controversy.

deposit date the date the PTO receives a patent application.

deposition oral or written testimony of a party or witness and given under oath.

design patent covers the unique, ornamental, or visible shape or design of a non-natural object.

divisional application a patent application used when an applicant wants to protect several inventions claimed in the original application. The official definition is "a later application for a distinct or independent invention, carved out of a pending application and disclosing and claiming only subject matter disclosed in the earlier or parent application" (MPEP 201.06). A divisional application is entitled to the filing date of the parent case for purposes of overcoming prior art. The divisional application must be filed while the parent is pending. A divisional application can be filed as a CPA.

Doctrine of Equivalents (DoE) a form of patent infringement that occurs when an invention performs substantially the same function in substantially the same manner and obtains the same result as the patented invention. A court analyzes each element of the patented invention separately. Under a recent Supreme Court decision, the DoE must be applied on an element-by-element basis to the claims.

double patenting when an applicant has obtained a patent and has filed a second application containing the same invention, the second application will be rejected. If the second application resulted in a patent, that patent will be invalidated. Two applications contain the same invention when the two inventions are literally the same or the second invention is an obvious modification of the first invention.

enhanced damages (treble damages) in exceptional infringement cases, financial damages may be increased, at the discretion of the court, up to triple the award for actual damages (known as "enhanced damages").

exclusive jurisdiction the sole authority of a court to hear a certain type of case.

exhaustion (see "first sale doctrine").

experimental use doctrine a rule excusing an inventor from the one-year bar provided that the alleged sale or public use was primarily for the purpose of perfecting or testing the invention.

file wrapper estoppel (or prosecution history estoppel) affirmative defense used in patent infringement litigation that precludes the patent owner from asserting rights that were disclaimed during the patent application process. The term is derived from the fact that the official file in which a patent is contained at the Patent and Trademark Office is known as a "file wrapper." All statements, admissions, correspondence, or documentation relating to the invention are placed in the file wrapper. Estoppel means that a party is prevented from acting contrary to a former statement or action when someone else has relied to his detriment on the prior statement or action.

final office action the examiner's response to the applicant's first amendment, The final Office Action is supposed to end the prosecution stage but a "final action" is rarely final.

first Office Action (sometimes called an "official letter" or "OA") response from the patent examiner after the initial examination of the application. It is very rare that an application is allowed in the first Office Action. More often, the examiner rejects some or all of the claims.

first sale doctrine (also known as the exhaustion doctrine) once a patented product (or product resulting from a patented process) is sold or licensed, the patent owner's rights are exhausted and the owner has no further rights as to the resale of that particular article.

indirect infringement occurs either when someone is persuaded to make, use, or sell a patented invention without authorization (inducing infringement); or when a material component of a patented invention is sold with knowledge that the component is designed for an unauthorized use (contributory infringement). An indirect infringement cannot occur unless there is a direct infringement. In other words, it is not enough to sell infringing parts; those parts must be used in an infringing invention.

infringement an invention is infringing if it is a literal copy of a patented invention or if it performs substantially the same function in substantially the same manner and obtains the same result as the patented invention (see "doctrine of equivalents").

injunction a court order requiring that a party halt a particular activity. In the case of patent infringement, a court can order all infringing activity be halted at the end of a trial (a permanent injunction) or the patent owner can attempt to halt the infringing activity immediately, rather than wait for a trial (a preliminary injunction). A court uses two factors to determine whether to grant a preliminary injunction: (1) Is the plaintiff likely to succeed in the lawsuit? and (2) Will the plaintiff suffer irreparable harm if the injunction is not granted? The patent owner may seek relief for a very short injunction known as a temporary restraining order or TRO, which usually only lasts a few days or weeks. A temporary restraining order may be granted without notice to the infringer if it appears that immediate damage will result—for example, that evidence will be destroyed.

interference a costly, complex PTO proceeding that determines who will get a patent when two or more applicants are claiming the same invention. It is basically a method of sorting out priority of inventorship. Occasionally an interference may involve a patent that has been in force for less than one year.

interrogatories written questions that must be answered under oath.

invention any new article, machine, composition, or process or new use developed by a human.

jury instructions explanations of the legal rules that the jury must use in reaching a verdict.

lab notebook a system of documenting an invention that usually includes descriptions of the invention and novel features; procedures used in the building and testing of the invention; drawings, photos, or sketches of the invention; test results and conclusions; discussions of any known prior-art references and additional documentation such as correspondence and purchase receipts.

literal infringement occurs if a defendant makes, sells, or uses the invention defined in the plaintiff's patent claim. In other words, the infringing product includes each and every component, part, or step in the patented invention. It is a literal infringement because the defendant's device is actually the *same* invention in the patent claim.

machine a device or things used for accomplishing a task; usually involves some activity or motion performed by working parts.

magistrate an officer of the court, who may exercise some of the authority of a federal district court judge, including the authority to conduct a jury or non-jury trial.

manufactures (sometimes termed "articles of manufacture") items that have been made by human hands or by machines; may have working or moving parts as prime features.

means-plus-function clause (or means for clause) a provision in a patent claim in which the applicant does not specifically describe the structure of one of the items in the patent and instead describes the function of the item. Term is derived from the fact that the clause usually starts with the word "means."

new matter any technical information, including dimensions, materials, etc., that was not present in the patent application as originally filed. An applicant can never add new matter to an application (PTO Rule 118).

new-use invention a new and unobvious process or method for using an old and known invention.

nonobviousness a standard of patentability that requires that an invention produce "unusual and surprising results." In 1966, the U.S. Supreme Court established the steps for determining unobviousness in the case of *Graham v. John Deere*, 383 US 1 (1966).

Notice of Allowance a document issued when the examiner is convinced that the application meets the requirements of patentability. An issue fee is due within three months.

objects and advantages a phrase used to explain "what the invention accomplishes." Usually, the objects are also the invention's advantages, since those aspects are intended to be superior over prior art.

Office Action (OA, also known as Official Letter or Examiner's Action) correspondence (usually including forms and a letter) from a patent examiner that describes what is wrong with the application and why it cannot be allowed. Generally, an OA will reject claims, list defects in the specifications or drawings, raise objections, or cite and enclose copies of relevant prior art demonstrating a lack of novelty or nonobviousness.

on-sale bar prevents an inventor from acquiring patent protection if the application is filed more than one year from the date of sale, use, or offer of sale of the invention in the United States.

one-year rule a rule that requires an inventor to file a patent application within one year after selling, offering for sale, or commercially or publicly using or describing an invention. If an inventor fails to file within one year of such occurrence the inventor is barred from obtaining a patent.

patent a grant from a government that confers upon an inventor the right to exclude others from making, using, selling, importing, or offering an invention for sale for a fixed period of time.

patent application a set of papers that describe an invention and that are suitable for filing in a patent office in order to apply for a patent on the invention.

Patent Application Declaration (PAD) a declaration that identifies the inventor or joint inventors and provides an attestation by the applicant that the inventor understands the contents of the claims and specification and has fully disclosed all material information. The PTO provides a form for the PAD.

patent misuse a defense in patent infringement that prevents a patent owner who has abused patent law from enforcing patent rights. Common examples of misuse are violation of the antitrust laws or unethical business practices.

patent pending (also known as the "pendency period") time between filing a patent application (or PPA) and issuance of the patent. The inventor has no patent rights during this period. However, when and if the patent later issues, the inventor will obtain the right to prevent the continuation of any infringing activity that started during the pendency period. If the application has been published by the PTO during the pendency period and the infringer had notice, the applicant may later seek royalties for these infringements during the pendency period. It's a criminal offense to use the words "patent applied for" or "patent pending" (they mean the same thing) in any advertising if there's no active, applicable regular or provisional patent application on file.

patent prosecution the process of shepherding a patent application through the Patent and Trademark Office.

Patent Rules of Practice administrative regulations located in Volume 37 of the Code of Federal Regulations (37 CFR § 1).

pendency period (see patent pending).

permanent injunction a durable injunction issued after a final judgment on the merits of the case; permanently restrains the defendant from engaging in the infringing activity.

Petition to Make Special an applicant can, under certain circumstances, have an application examined sooner than the normal course of PTO examination (one to three years). This is accomplished by filing a "Petition to Make Special" (PTMS), together with a Supporting Declaration.

plant patent covers plants that can be reproduced through the use of grafts and cuttings (asexual reproduction).

power of attorney a document that gives another person legal authority to act on your behalf. If an attorney is preparing an application on behalf of an inventor, a power of attorney should be executed to authorize the patent attorney or agent to act on behalf of the inventor. The power of attorney form may be combined with the PAD.

prior art the state of knowledge existing or publicly available either before the date of an invention or more than one year prior to the patent application date.

process (sometimes referred to as a "method") a way of doing or making things that involves more than purely mental manipulations.

Provisional Patent Application (PPA) an interim document that clearly explains how to make and use the invention. The PPA is equivalent to a reduction to practice (see below). If a regular patent application is filed within one year of filing the PPA, the inventor can use the PPA's filing date for the purpose of deciding whether a reference is prior art. In addition to an early filing date, an inventor may claim patent pending status for the one-year period following the filing of PPA.

reduction to practice the point at which the inventor can demonstrate that the invention works for its intended purpose. Reduction to practice can be accomplished by building and testing the invention (actual reduction to practice) or by preparing a patent application or provisional patent application that shows how to make and use the invention and that it works (constructive reduction practice). In the event of a dispute or a challenge at the PTO, invention documentation is essential in order to prove the "how and when" of conception and reduction to practice.

reissue application an application used to correct information in a patent. It is usually filed when a patent owner believes the claims are not broad enough, the claims are too broad (the applicant discovered a new reference), or there are significant errors in the specification. In these cases, the applicant seeks to correct the patent by filing an application to get the applicant's original patent reissued at any time during its term. The reissue patent will take the place of the applicant's original patent and expire the same time as the original patent would have expired. If the applicant wants to broaden the claims of the patent through a reissue application, the applicant must do so within two years from the date the original patent issued. There is a risk in filing a reissue application because all of the claims of the original patent will be examined and can be rejected.

repair doctrine affirmative defense based on the right of an authorized licensor of a patented device to repair and replace unpatented components. It also includes the right to sell materials used to repair or replace a patented invention The defense does not apply for completely rebuilt inventions, unauthorized inventions, or items that are made or sold without authorization of the patent owner.

request for admission request for a party to the lawsuit to admit the truthfulness of a statement.

Request for Continued Examination (RCE) a paper filed when a patent applicant wishes to continue prosecuting an application that has received a final **Office Action**. Filing the RCE with another filing fee effectively removes the final action so that the applicant can submit further amendments, for example, new claims, new arguments, a new declaration, or new references.

request for production of documents the way a party to a lawsuit obtains documents or other physical evidence from the other side.

reverse doctrine of equivalents (or negative doctrine of equivalents) a rarely used affirmative defense to patent infringement in

which, even if there is a literal infringement, the court will excuse the defendant's conduct if the infringing device has a different function or result than the patented invention. The doctrine is applied when the allegedly infringing device performs the same function in a substantially different way.

sequence listing an attachment to a patent application used if a biotech invention includes a sequence listing of a nucleotide or amino acid sequence. The applicant attaches this information on separate sheets of paper and refers to the sequence listing in the application (see PTO Rule 77). If there is no sequence listing, the applicant states "Non applicable."

Small Entity Status a status that enables small businesses, independent inventors, and non-profit companies to pay a reduced application fee. There are three types of small entities: (1) independent inventors, (2) non-profit companies, and (3) small businesses. To qualify, an independent inventor must either own all rights, or have transferred—or be obligated to transfer—rights to a small business or nonprofit organization. Nonprofit organizations are defined and listed in the Code of Federal Regulations and usually are educational institutions or charitable organizations. A small entity business is one with fewer than 500 employees. The number of employees is computed by averaging the number of full- and part-time employees during a fiscal year.

specification a patent application disclosure made by the inventor and drafted so that an individual skilled in the art to which the invention pertains could, when reading the patent, make and use the invention without needing further experiment. A **specification** is constructed of several sections. Collectively, these sections form a narrative that describes and distinguishes the invention. If it can later be proved that the inventor knew of a better way (or "best mode") and failed to disclose it, that failure could result in the loss of patent rights.

statute of limitations the legally prescribed time limit in which a lawsuit must be filed. In patent law there is no time limit (statute of limitations) for filing a patent infringement lawsuit, but monetary damages can only be recovered for infringements committed during the six years prior to the filing the lawsuit. For example if a patent owner sues after ten years of infringement, the owner cannot recover monetary damages for the first four years of infringement. Despite the fact that there is no law setting a time limit, courts will not permit a patent owner to sue for infringement if the owner has waited an unreasonable time to file the lawsuit ("laches").

Statutory Invention Registration (SIR) a document that allows an applicant who abandons an application to prevent anyone else from getting a valid patent on the same invention. This is accomplished by converting the patent application to a SIR.

statutory subject matter an invention that falls into one of the five statutory classes: process (method), machine, article of manufacture, composition, or a "new use" of one of the first four.

substitute application essentially a duplicate of an abandoned patent application. (See MPEP 201.09). The disadvantage of a substitute application is that the applicant doesn't get the benefit of the filing date of the previously abandoned patent application, which could be useful because any prior art occurring after the filing date of the earlier case can be used against the substitute case. If the applicant's substitute application issues into a patent, the patent will expire 20 years from the filing date of the substitute.

successor liability responsibility for infringement that is borne by a company that has purchased another company that is liable for infringements. In order for successor liability to occur, there must be an agreement between the companies to assume liability, a merger between the companies, or the purchaser must be a "continuation" of the purchased business. If the sale is made to escape liability and lacks any of the foregoing characteristics, liability will still attach.

summons a document served with the complaint that tells the defendant he has been sued, has a certain time limit in which to respond, and must appear in court on a stated date.

temporary restraining order (TRO) a court order that tells one party to do or stop doing something—for example to stop infringing. A TRO is issued after the aggrieved party appears before a judge. Once the TRO is issued, the court holds a second hearing where the other side can tell his story and the court can decide whether to make the TRO permanent by issuing an injunction. The TRO is often granted *ex parte* (without allowing the other side to respond), and for that reason is short in duration and only remains in effect until the court has an opportunity to schedule a hearing for the preliminary injunction.

tying a form of patent misuse in which, as a condition of a transaction, the buyer of a patented device must also purchase an additional product. For example, in one case a company had a patent on a machine that deposited salt tablets in canned food.

Purchasers of the machine were also required to buy salt tablets from the patent owner. A party that commits patent misuse may have its patent invalidated, may have to pay monetary damages, or both.

utility patent the main type of patent, which covers inventions that function in a unique manner to produce a utilitarian result.

vicarious liability legal responsibility that results when a business such as a corporation or partnership is liable for infringements committed by employees or agents. This liability attaches when the agent acts under the authority or direction of the business, an employee acts within the scope of employment, or the business benefits from, or adopts or approves the infringing activity.

voir dire *("speak the truth")* process by which attorneys and judges question potential jurors in order to determine whether they may be fair and impartial. ■

Index

Remember:

Little publishers have big ears.
We really listen to you.

Take 2 Minutes & Give Us Your 2 cents

Your comments make a big difference in the development and revision of Nolo books and software. Please take a few minutes and register your Nolo product—and your comments—with us. Not only will your input make a difference, you'll receive special offers available only to registered owners of Nolo products on our newest books and software. Register now by:

PHONE
1-800-728-3555

FAX
1-800-645-0895

EMAIL
cs@nolo.com

or **MAIL** us
this registration card

------------------------------- fold here -------------------------------

Registration Card

NAME _____ DATE _____

ADDRESS _____

_____

CITY _____ STATE _____ ZIP _____

PHONE _____ EMAIL _____

WHERE DID YOU HEAR ABOUT THIS PRODUCT? _____

WHERE DID YOU PURCHASE THIS PRODUCT? _____

DID YOU CONSULT A LAWYER? (PLEASE CIRCLE ONE)   YES   NO   NOT APPLICABLE

DID YOU FIND THIS BOOK HELPFUL?   (VERY)   5   4   3   2   1   (NOT AT ALL)

COMMENTS _____

_____

_____

WAS IT EASY TO USE?   (VERY EASY)   5   4   3   2   1   (VERY DIFFICULT)

We occasionally make our mailing list available to carefully selected companies whose products may be of interest to you.

❑ If you do not wish to receive mailings from these companies, please check this box.

❑ You can quote me in future Nolo promotional materials.
    Daytime phone number _____ .

QPAT 3.0

Nolo *in the* **NEWS**

"Nolo helps lay people perform legal tasks without the aid—or fees—of lawyers."
—USA TODAY

Nolo books are ..."written in plain language, free of legal mumbo jumbo, and spiced with witty personal observations."
—ASSOCIATED PRESS

"...Nolo publications...guide people simply through the how, when, where and why of law."
—WASHINGTON POST

"Increasingly, people who are not lawyers are performing tasks usually regarded as legal work... And consumers, using books like Nolo's, do routine legal work themselves."
—NEW YORK TIMES

"...All of [Nolo's] books are easy-to-understand, are updated regularly, provide pull-out forms...and are often quite moving in their sense of compassion for the struggles of the lay reader."
—SAN FRANCISCO CHRONICLE

fold here

- -

Nolo
950 Parker Street
Berkeley, CA 94710-9867

Attn: QPAT 3.0